COLOR THE CATS

Forty Real Cats From Around The World and Their Stories

I0478921

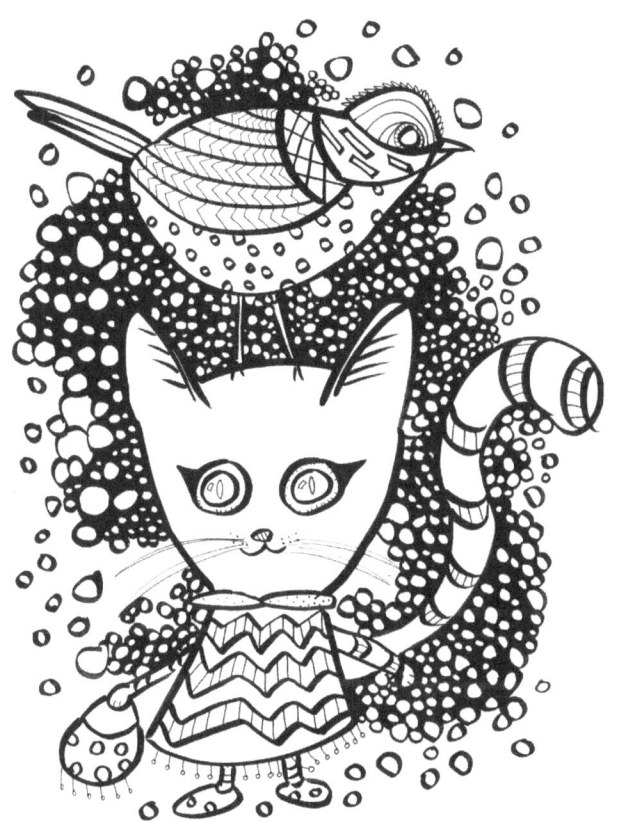

NEPETA ENTERPRISES LLC

GILBERTSVILLE PENNSYLVANIA

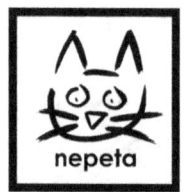

NEPETA PRESS
A DIVISION OF NEPETA ENTERPRISES LLC
P.O. BOX 314
POTTSTOWN, PA 19464

COPYEDITOR: DIANE MOSER
ART: PAMELA HODGES
COVER DESIGN: PAMELA HODGES
BOOK DESIGN: PAMELA HODGES
LITTER BOX CLEANER: PAMELA HODGES

PUBLISHED IN THE UNITED STATES BY NEPETA PRESS

TRADE PAPERBACK ISBN-13:978-1-941266-11-3

Introducing the Cats

This is a non-fiction coloring book. Each drawing and story is of a real cat.

The cats in this coloring book come from all over the world. They are from Australia, Canada, Denmark, France, Japan, the Philippines, South Africa, and the United States.

They have been rescued from busy highways in Dallas, Manila, and Moberly. The cats have been plucked from snow banks, garbage dumps, and rescue centers. And some of the cats just walked in the back door.

Coloring is Good For You

Coloring can calm the spirit and give rest to the soul. This coloring book is for children of all ages. Adults are really children with bigger feet. An adult may know how to drive a car and they might have a job and a mortgage, but deep down inside is a child who misses holding a crayon and coloring in a coloring book.

How to Color – in Case You Forgot

1. You can color inside the lines, or you can color outside the lines.
2. You can color realistically, or you can make your cat lime-green.
3. You can press hard or lightly with your crayon.
4. If you break a crayon, just peel off the paper and use the smaller piece.

Supplies Needed:

1. A coloring book (hopefully this one).
2. Crayons or pencil crayons.
3. If you use felt pens or colored markers, put a thick piece of scrap paper under the picture you are coloring so it won't bleed through the paper.

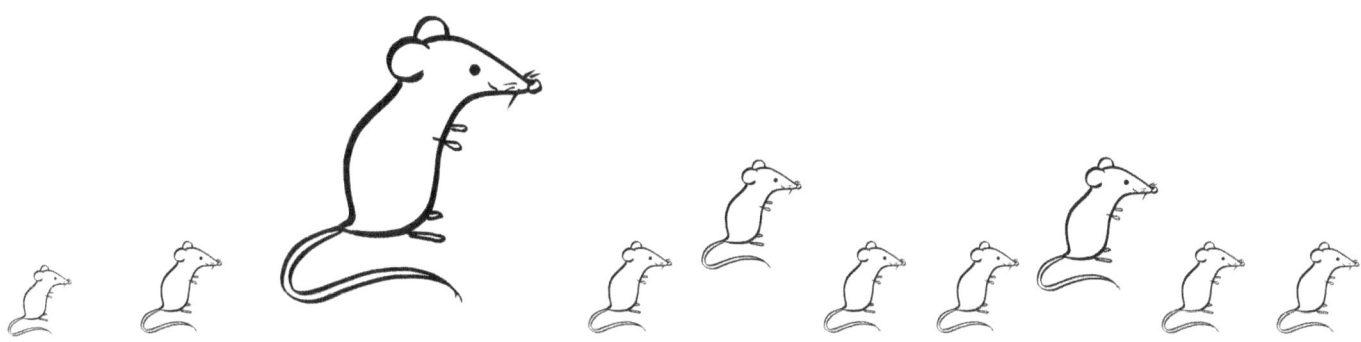

We are little mice. We are hiding from the cats. You can color us too.

cat - kat - gato- neko

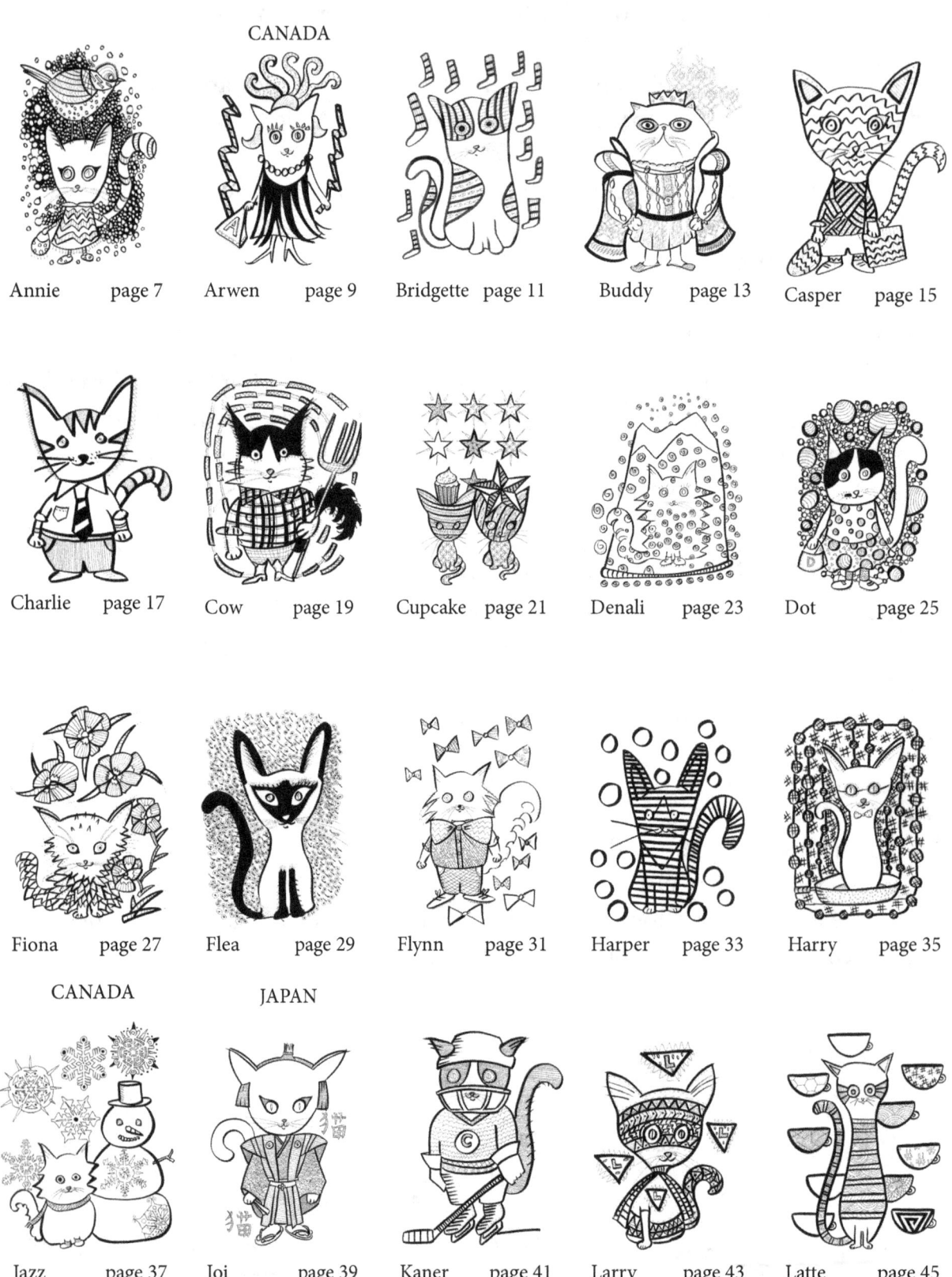

CANADA

Annie   page 7

Arwen   page 9

Bridgette   page 11

Buddy   page 13

Casper   page 15

Charlie   page 17

Cow   page 19

Cupcake   page 21

Denali   page 23

Dot   page 25

Fiona   page 27

Flea   page 29

Flynn   page 31

Harper   page 33

Harry   page 35

CANADA   JAPAN

Jazz   page 37

Joi   page 39

Kaner   page 41

Larry   page 43

Latte   page 45

All the other cats are from the United States of America, or USA.

chat - katt- pusa - kats

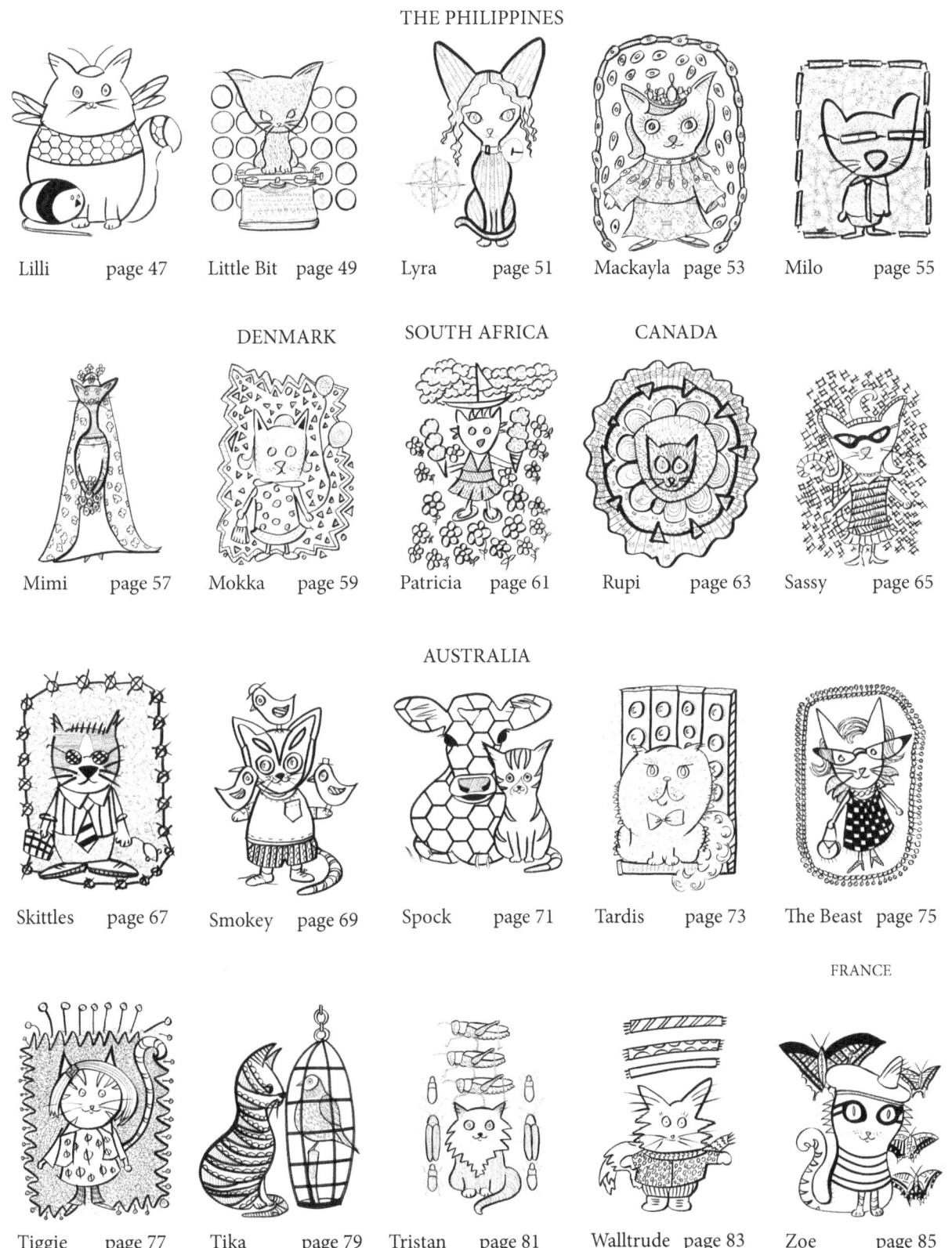

THE PHILIPPINES

Lilli page 47	Little Bit page 49	Lyra page 51	Mackayla page 53	Milo page 55

DENMARK   SOUTH AFRICA   CANADA

Mimi page 57	Mokka page 59	Patricia page 61	Rupi page 63	Sassy page 65

AUSTRALIA

Skittles page 67	Smokey page 69	Spock page 71	Tardis page 73	The Beast page 75

FRANCE

Tiggie page 77	Tika page 79	Tristan page 81	Walltrude page 83	Zoe page 85

All of these cats are real cats with real stories.

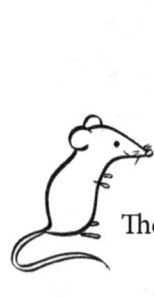 There are no cats on the back of this page, just me, a mouse. Please don't tell the cats I am here.

ANNIE

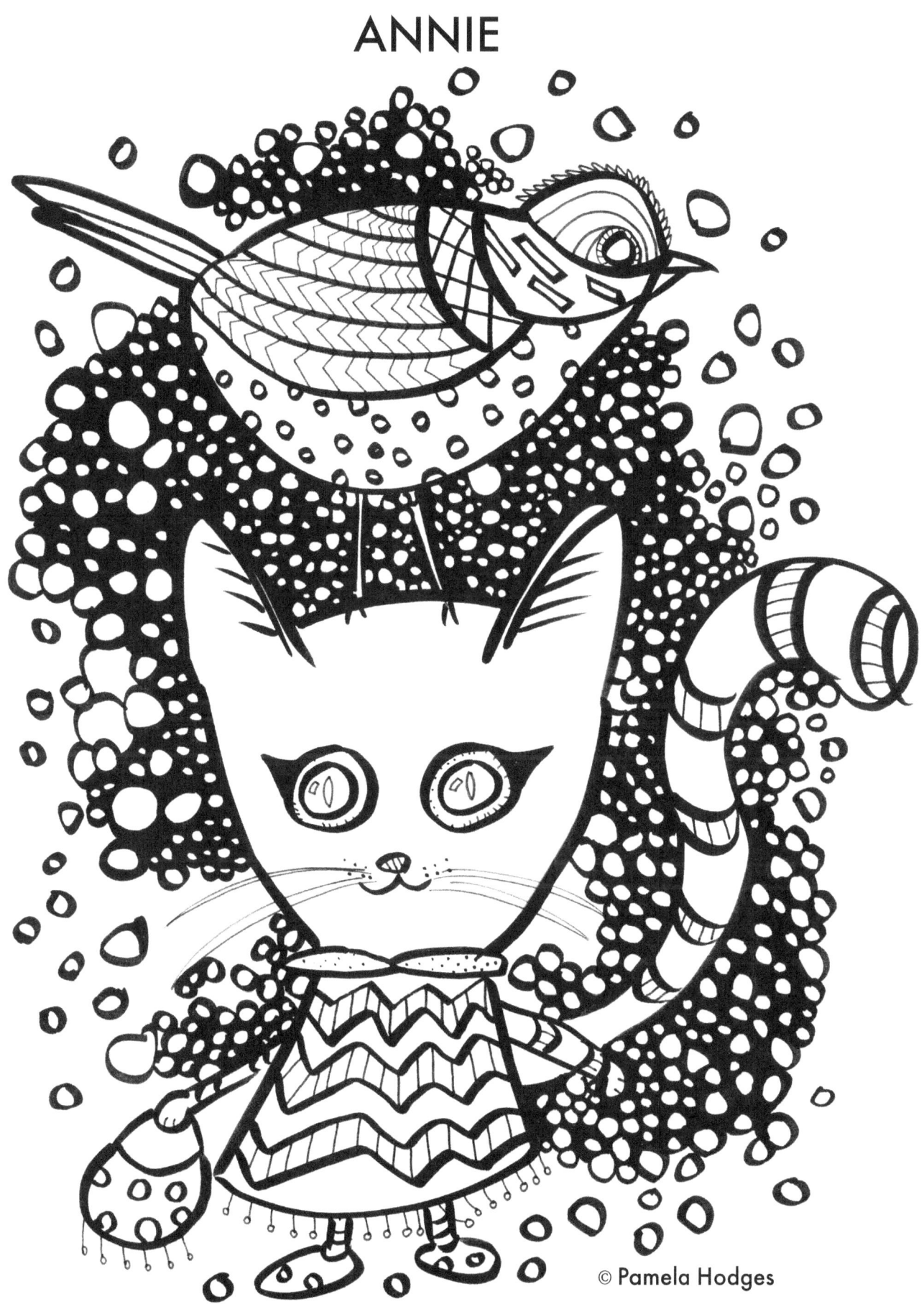

© Pamela Hodges

I used to live in a mobile home park until I got kicked out because of the no pet rules. My new mom and I love to watch the Black Headed Grosbeaks and the Townsends Warblers that come to our window. I am learning to get along with her dog, Jimmy, who is very large.

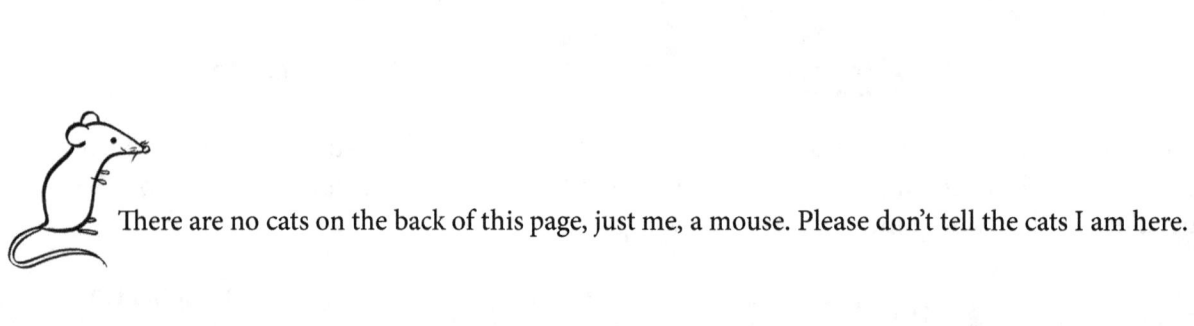 There are no cats on the back of this page, just me, a mouse. Please don't tell the cats I am here.

ARWEN

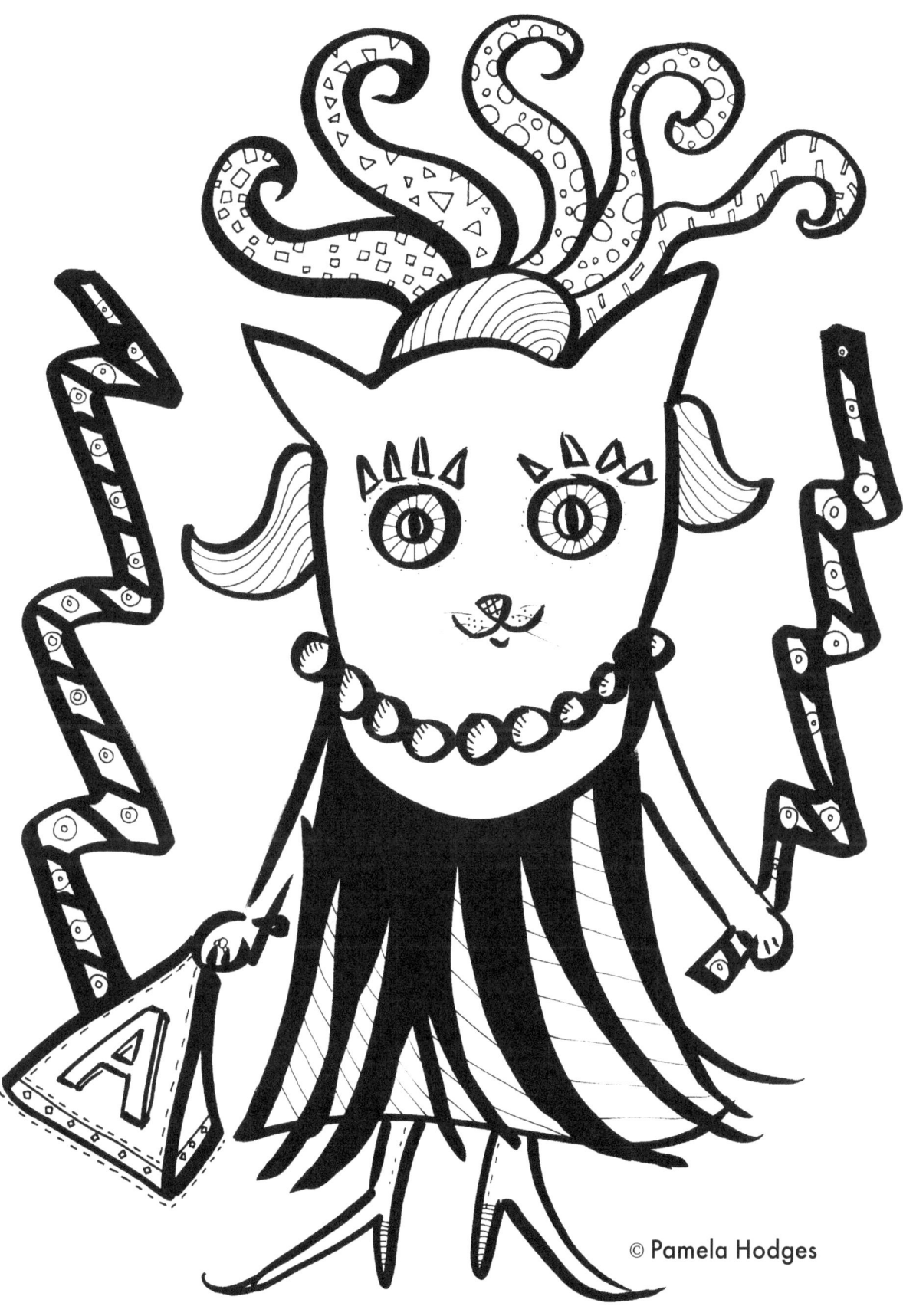

My human mother's cat, Sumo, died just four days after she moved to Halifax, Nova Scotia, Canada. Then she saw me, Arwen, at the Nova Scotia SPCA. And she said, "I have to rescue you. You look just like my dearly departed Sumo." I am still my mother's best friend.

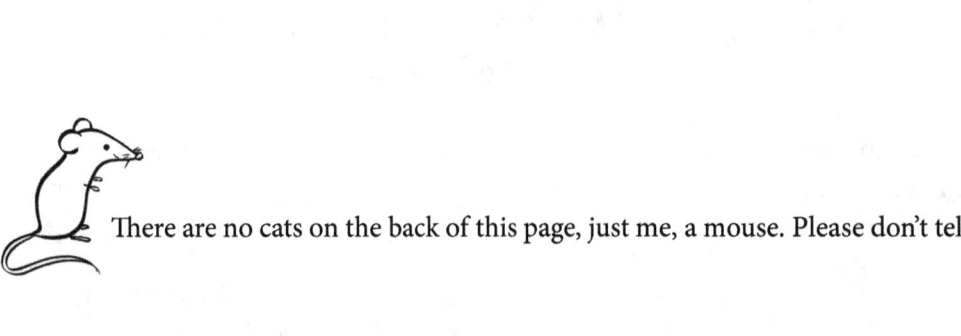 There are no cats on the back of this page, just me, a mouse. Please don't tell the cats I am here.

BRIDGETT

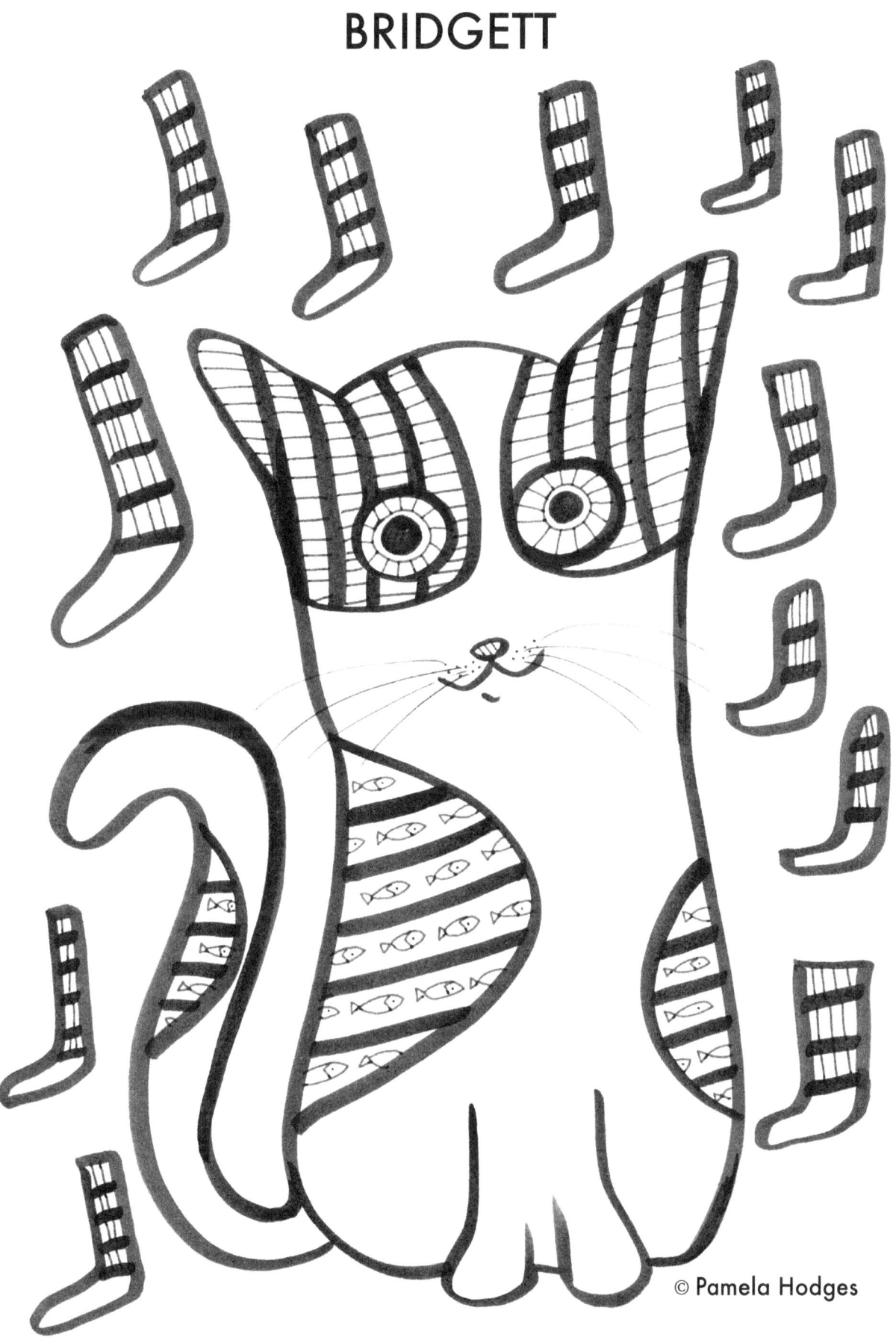

My name is Bridgett, and I love to steal socks. Five years ago some children found me in the gutter in the middle of winter in Idaho and took me home. I am so happy to be loved.

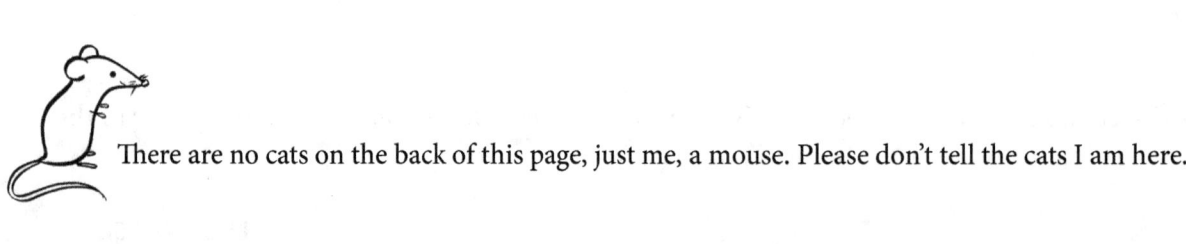

There are no cats on the back of this page, just me, a mouse. Please don't tell the cats I am here.

BUDDY

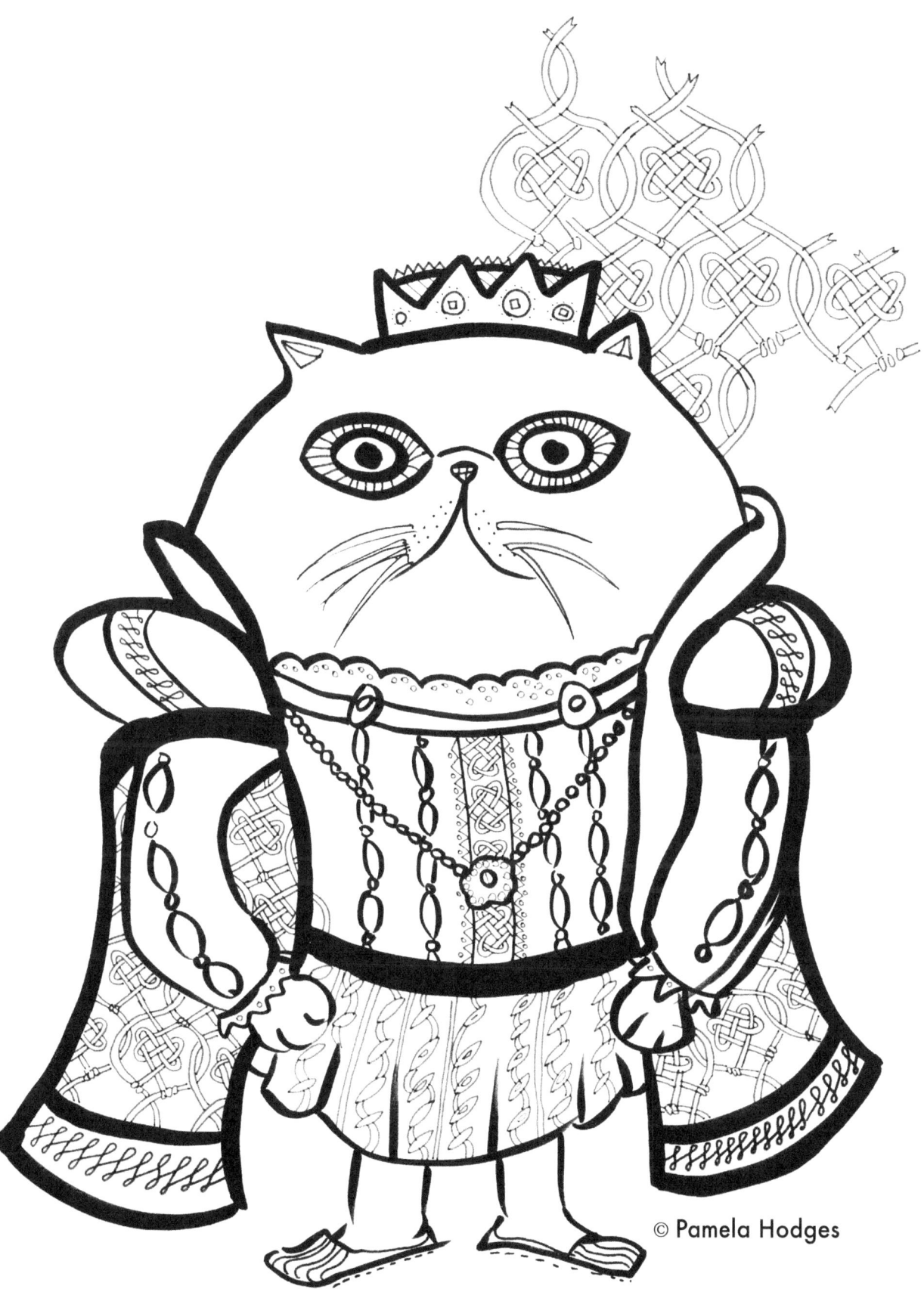

© Pamela Hodges

Hello, my name is Buddy the Cat. I am a copper-eyed white Persian. I was born in my mommy's house and was a show cat until I decided I would rather be a lawyer like my human mommy. We study for the Bar Exam together.

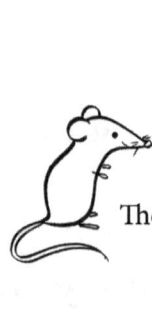 There are no cats on the back of this page, just me, a mouse. Please don't tell the cats I am here.

CASPER

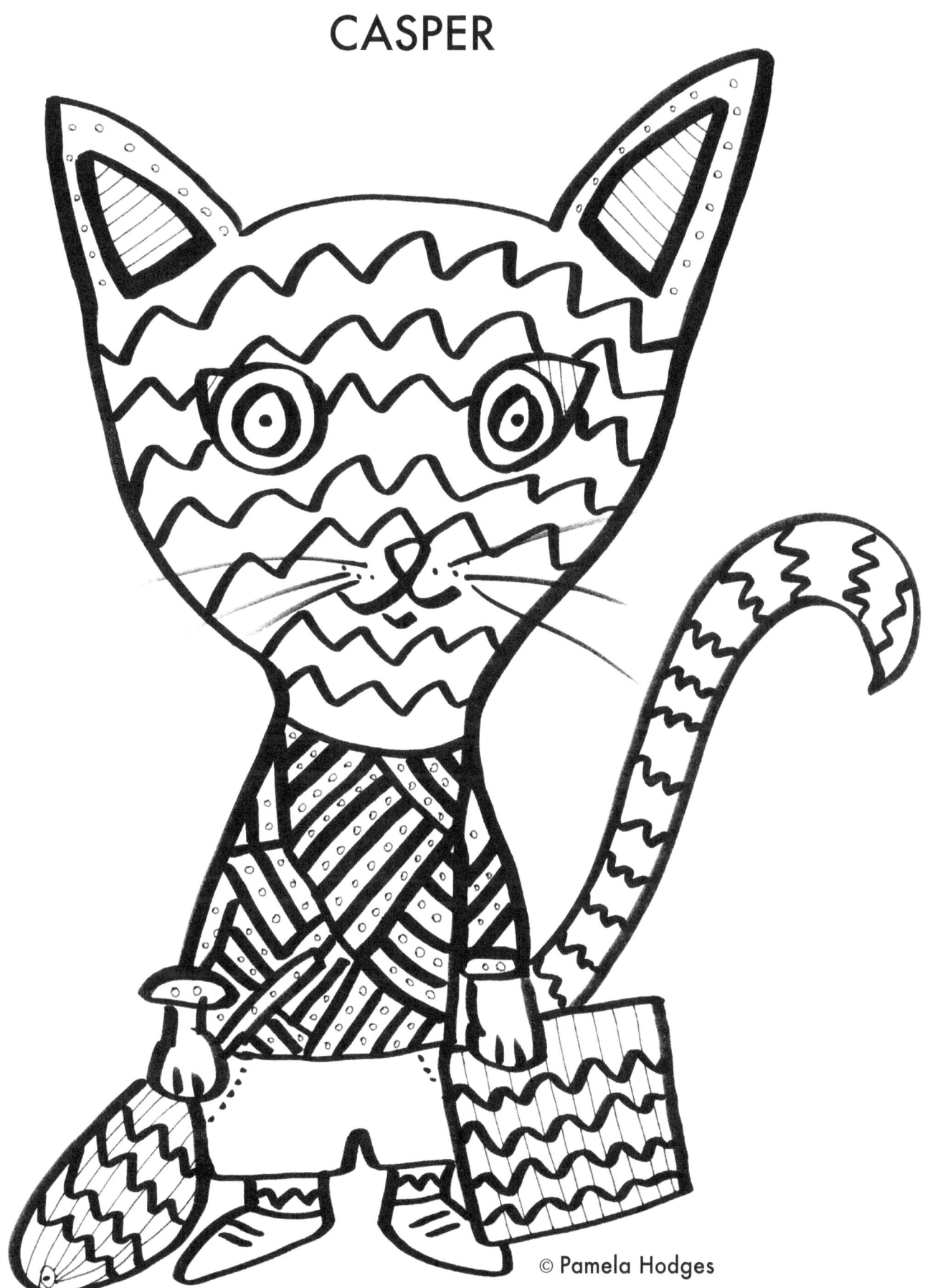

© Pamela Hodges

My name is Casper and I am a nurse. I stayed by Nana's side when she was ill. I used to live across the street from Nana, but there is a mean dog who lives there, and the dog was mean to my best friend, Kitty, so I never went back. I moved next door to Nana's house.

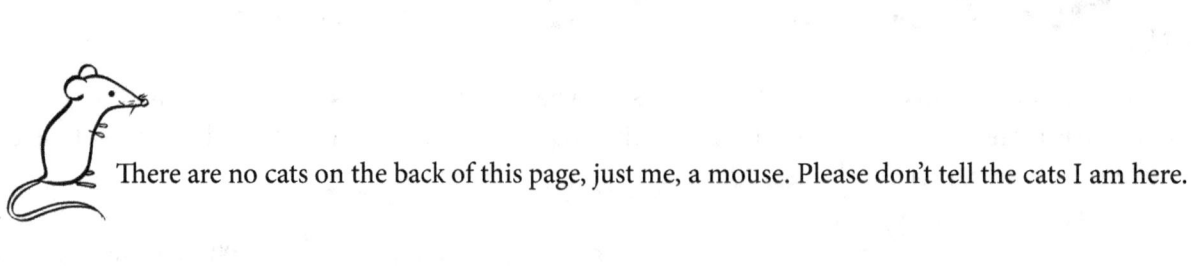 There are no cats on the back of this page, just me, a mouse. Please don't tell the cats I am here.

CHARLIE

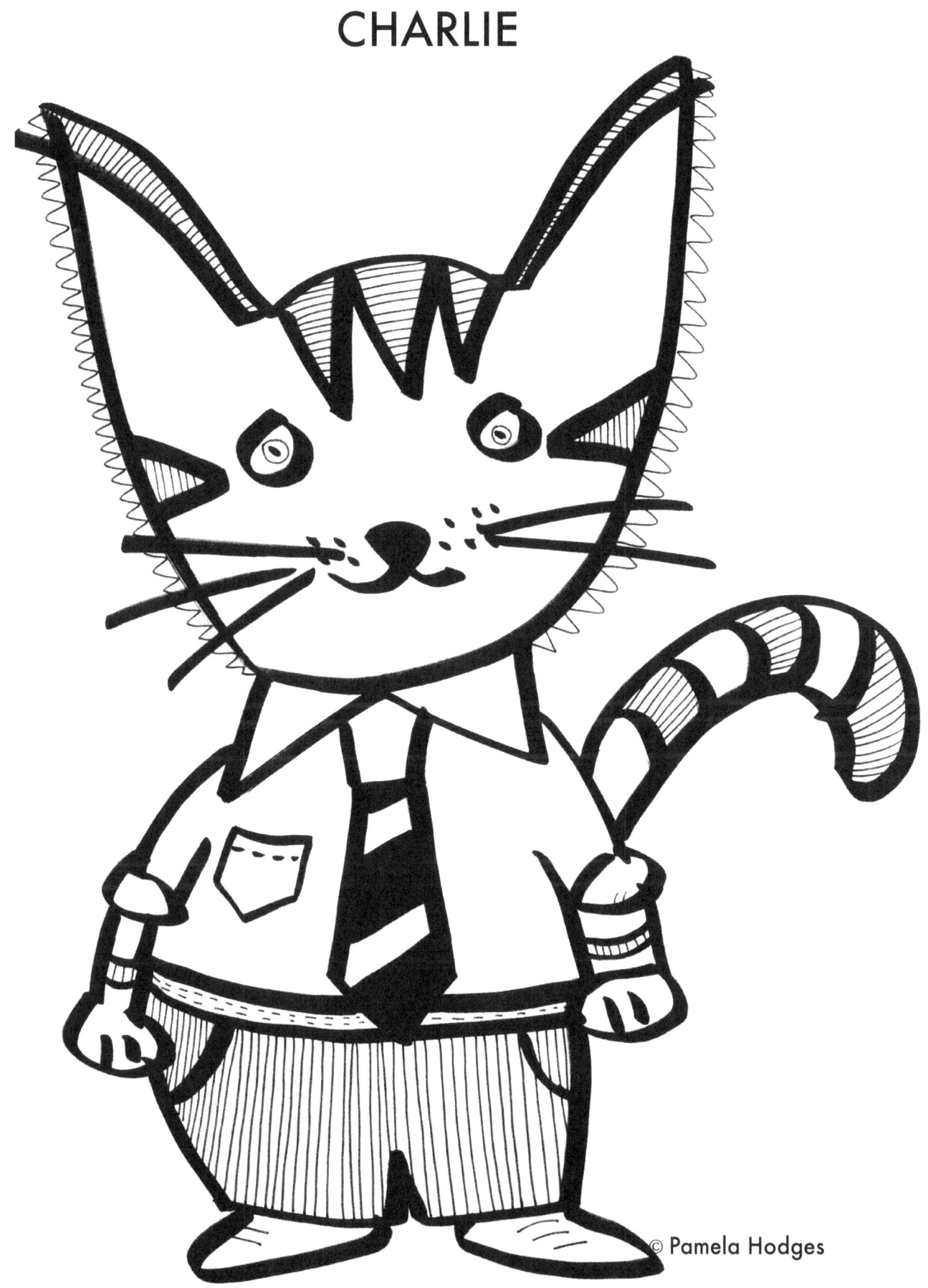

My favorite hobby is sleeping in a sunbeam. I also am in charge of dishwasher loading. I was rescued from an animal shelter in Pottstown, Pennsylvania. My rescuers named me Charlie. They almost named me Moon.

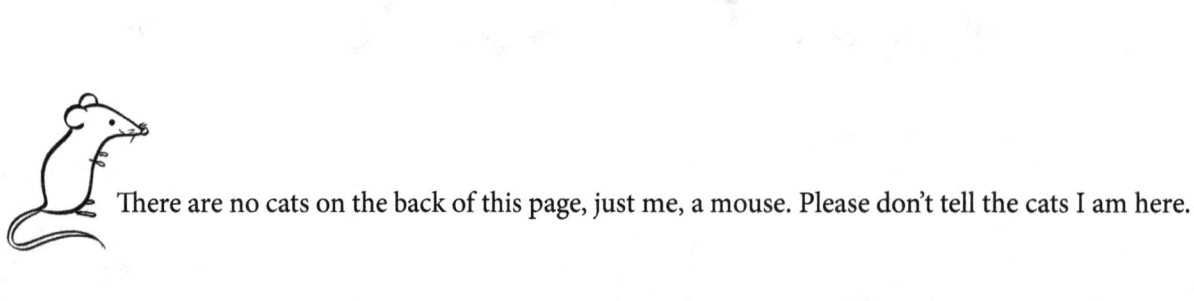
There are no cats on the back of this page, just me, a mouse. Please don't tell the cats I am here.

COW

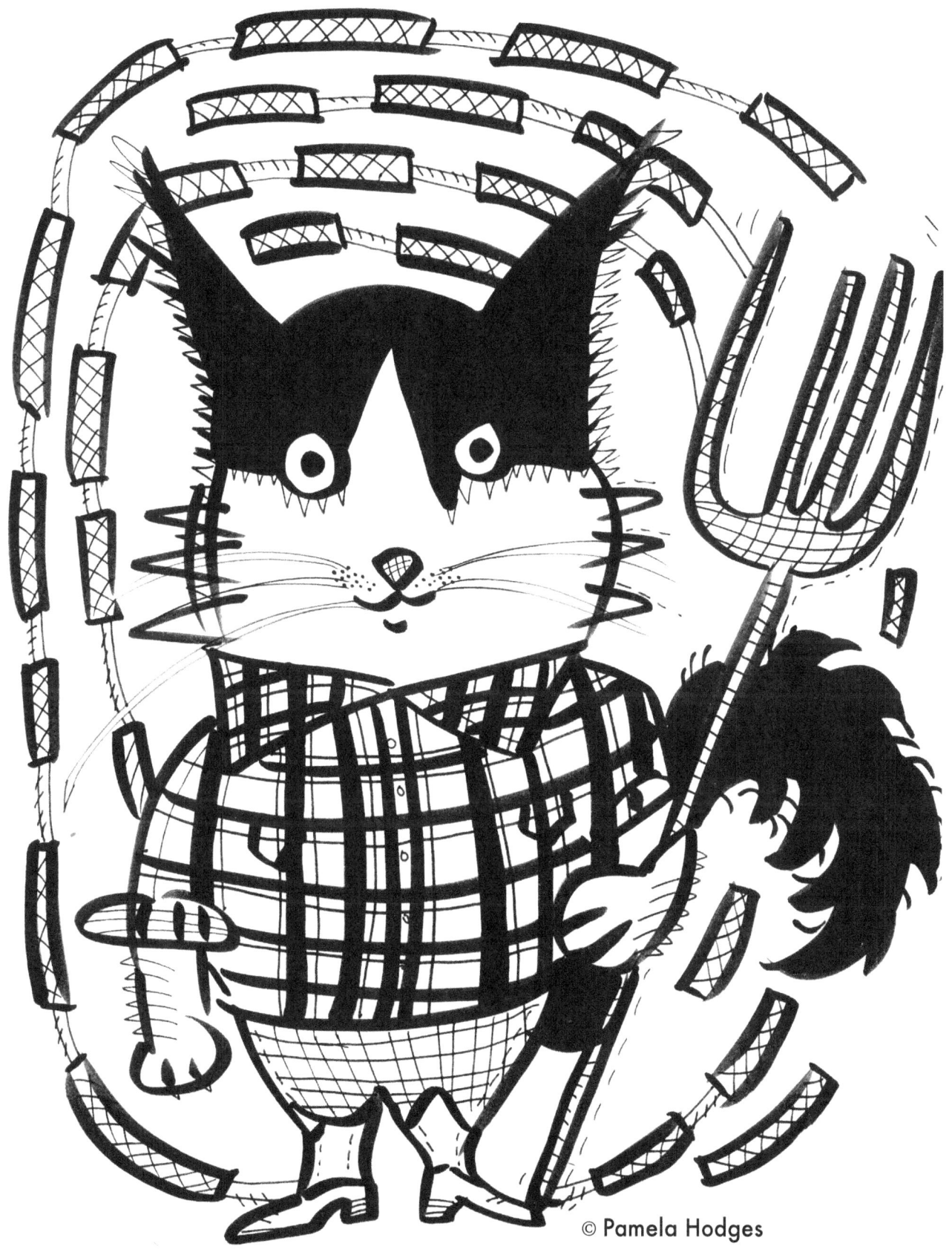

© Pamela Hodges

I showed up outside of a house in the summer of 2001. The people looked outside the window and said, "Look at that little cow cat out there," and the name stuck. I was already fixed and de-clawed and just needed a home. Now, I cuddle and greet people at the door.

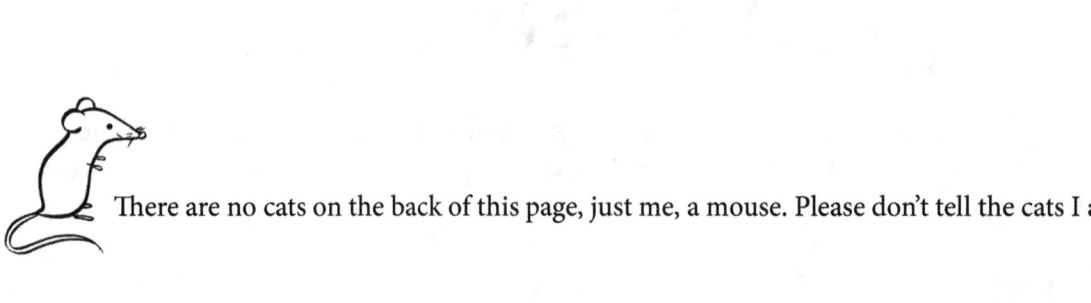 There are no cats on the back of this page, just me, a mouse. Please don't tell the cats I am here.

CUPCAKE AND STAR

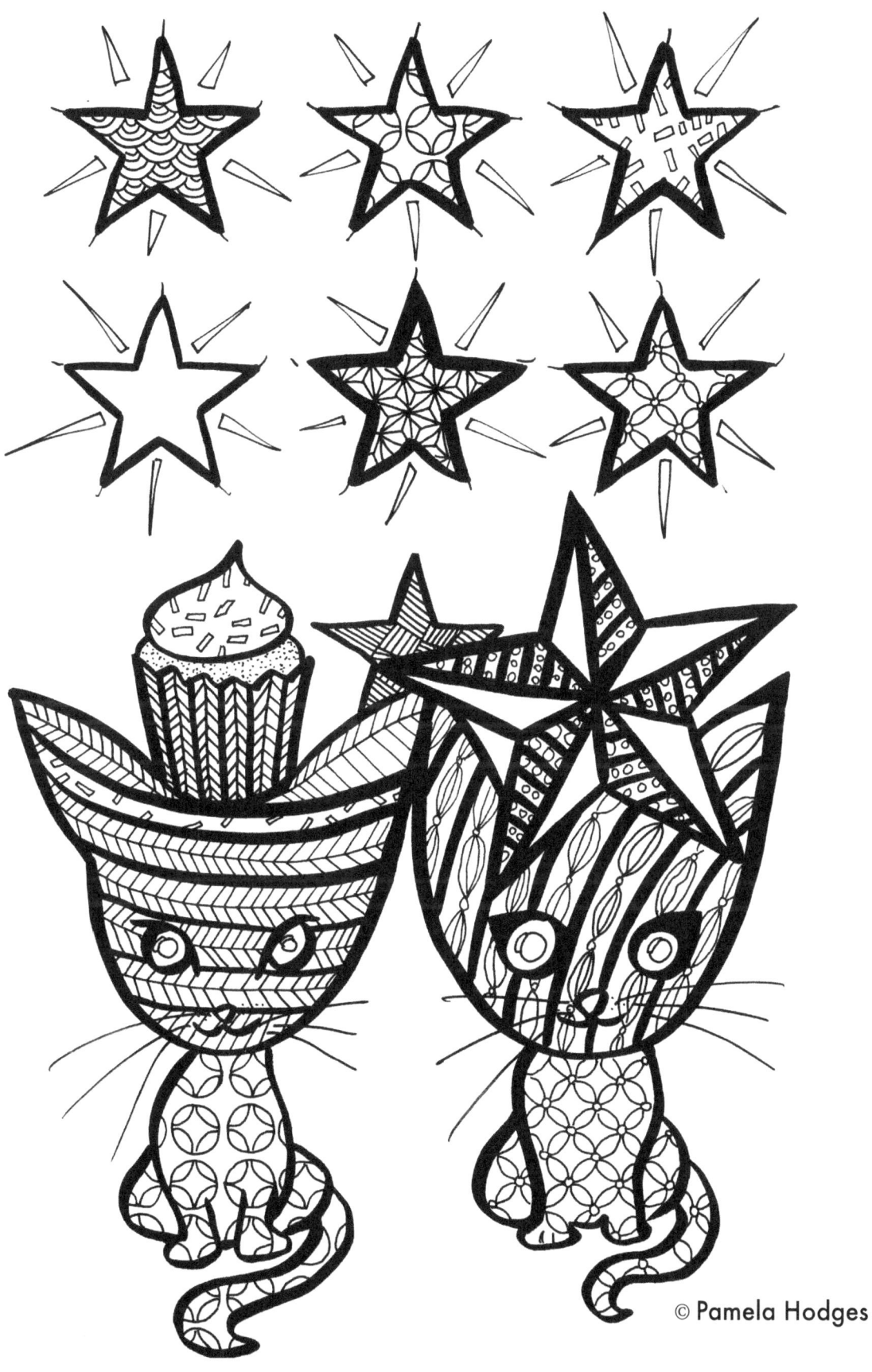

© Pamela Hodges

My sister, Star, and I were adopted together from a litter of kittens on Facebook. Our human mother had to wait six weeks until we were weaned before she could bring us home.

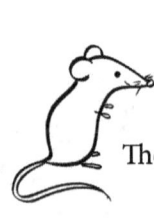 There are no cats on the back of this page, just me, a mouse. Please don't tell the cats I am here.

DENALI

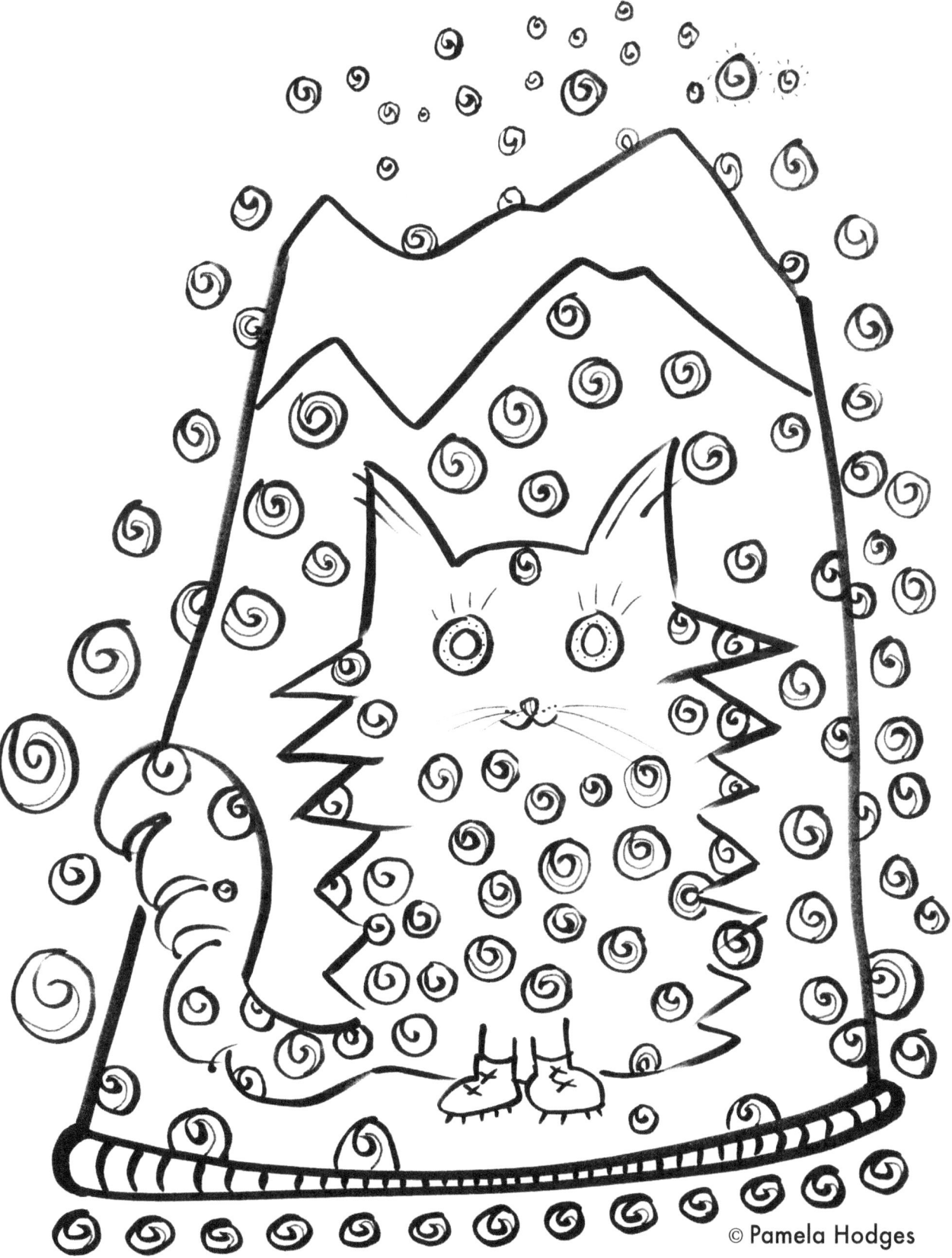

© Pamela Hodges

I certainly do enjoy scaling the sofa and tackling the plants I can reach from the top. I have already evaded death once by being rescued from a cat prison where my time was limited and my sentence severe. I am mischievous and always on the hunt for adventure, which is why they named me Denali.

 There are no cats on the back of this page, just me, a mouse. Please don't tell the cats I am here.

DOT

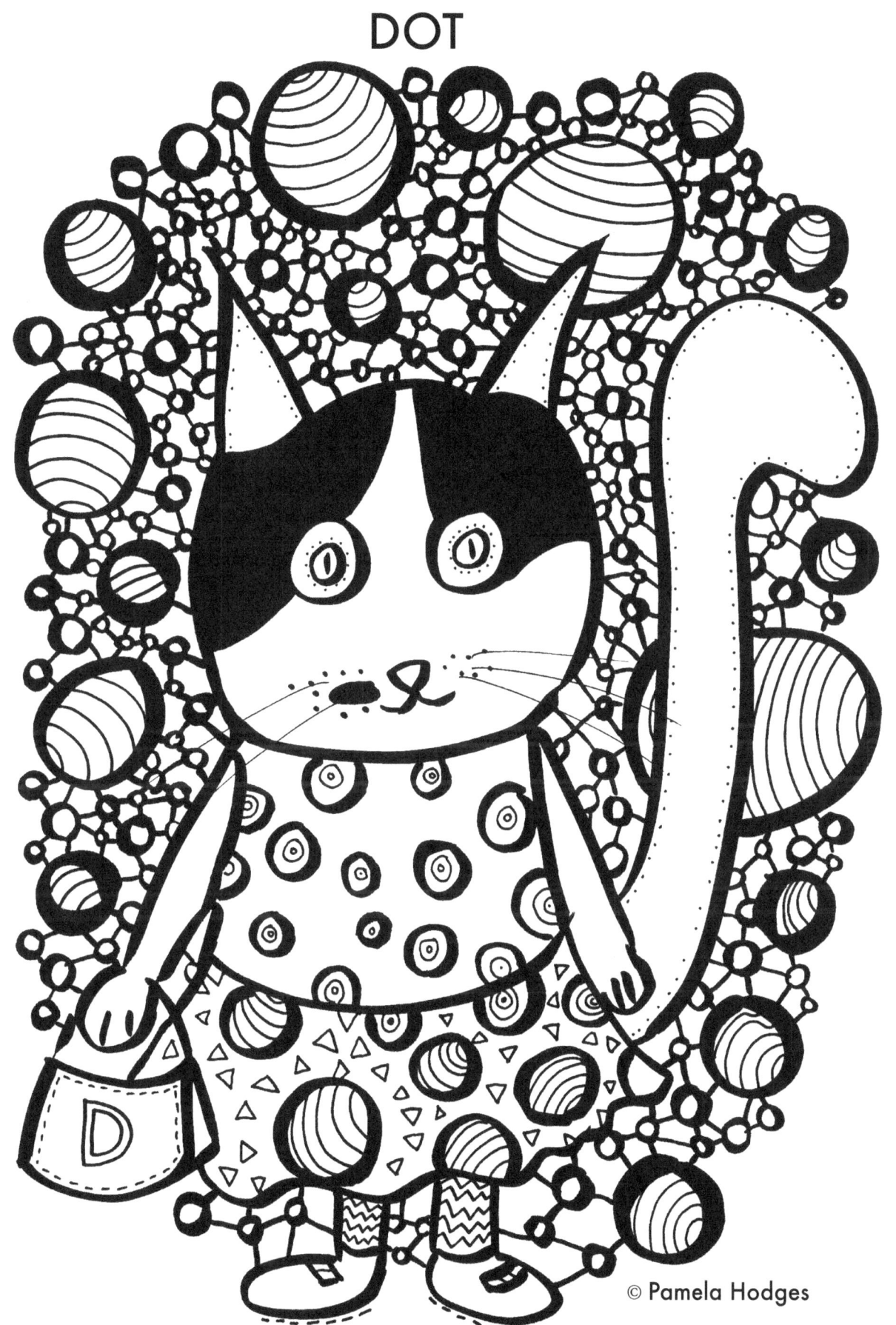

© Pamela Hodges

My name is Dot and I was adopted from Craig's List. I had been abandoned and the person who found me had other pets and couldn't add more to her household, so she put me up on Craig's list. I love my new family, especially the little girl who lives here.

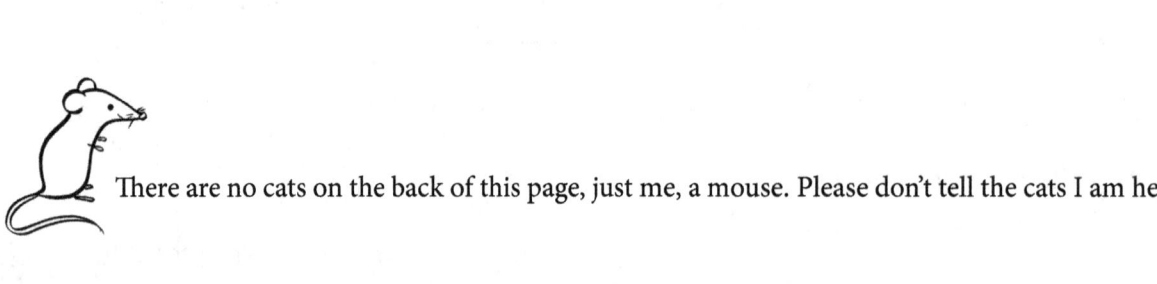
There are no cats on the back of this page, just me, a mouse. Please don't tell the cats I am here.

FIONA

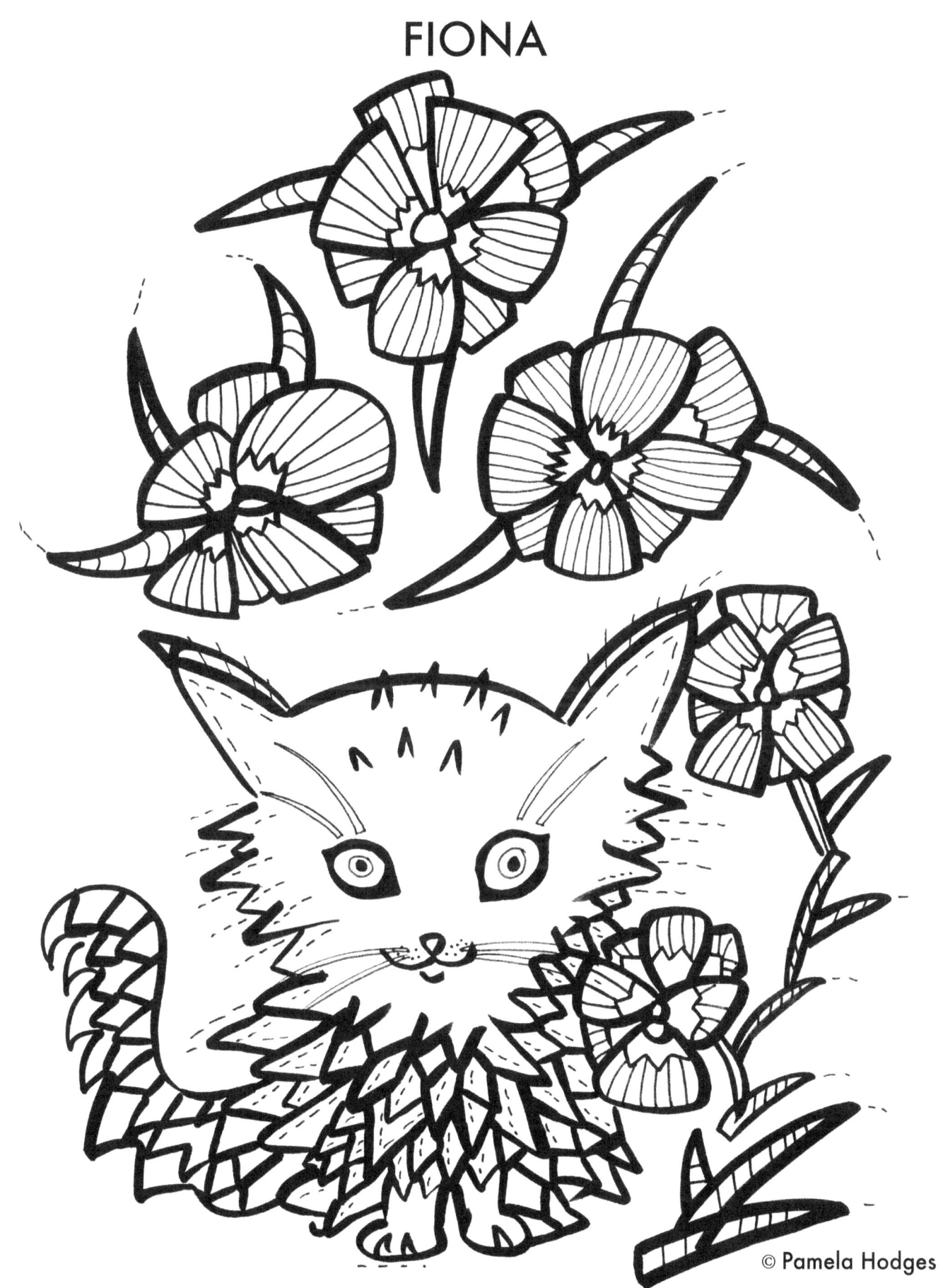

© Pamela Hodges

I like to take long walks to the neighbors where they feed me yummier food than where I live. I am undecided about my future career goals; however, no matter what I do as a career, I will always take time to smell the flowers, and come home to my mommy.

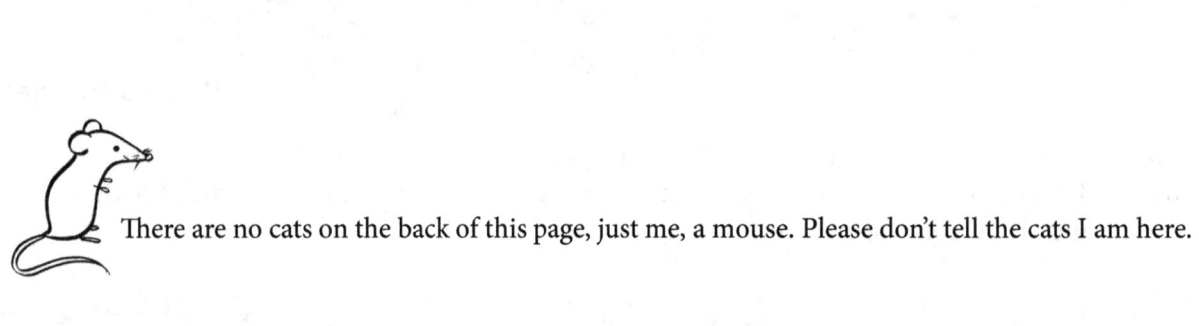 There are no cats on the back of this page, just me, a mouse. Please don't tell the cats I am here.

FLEA

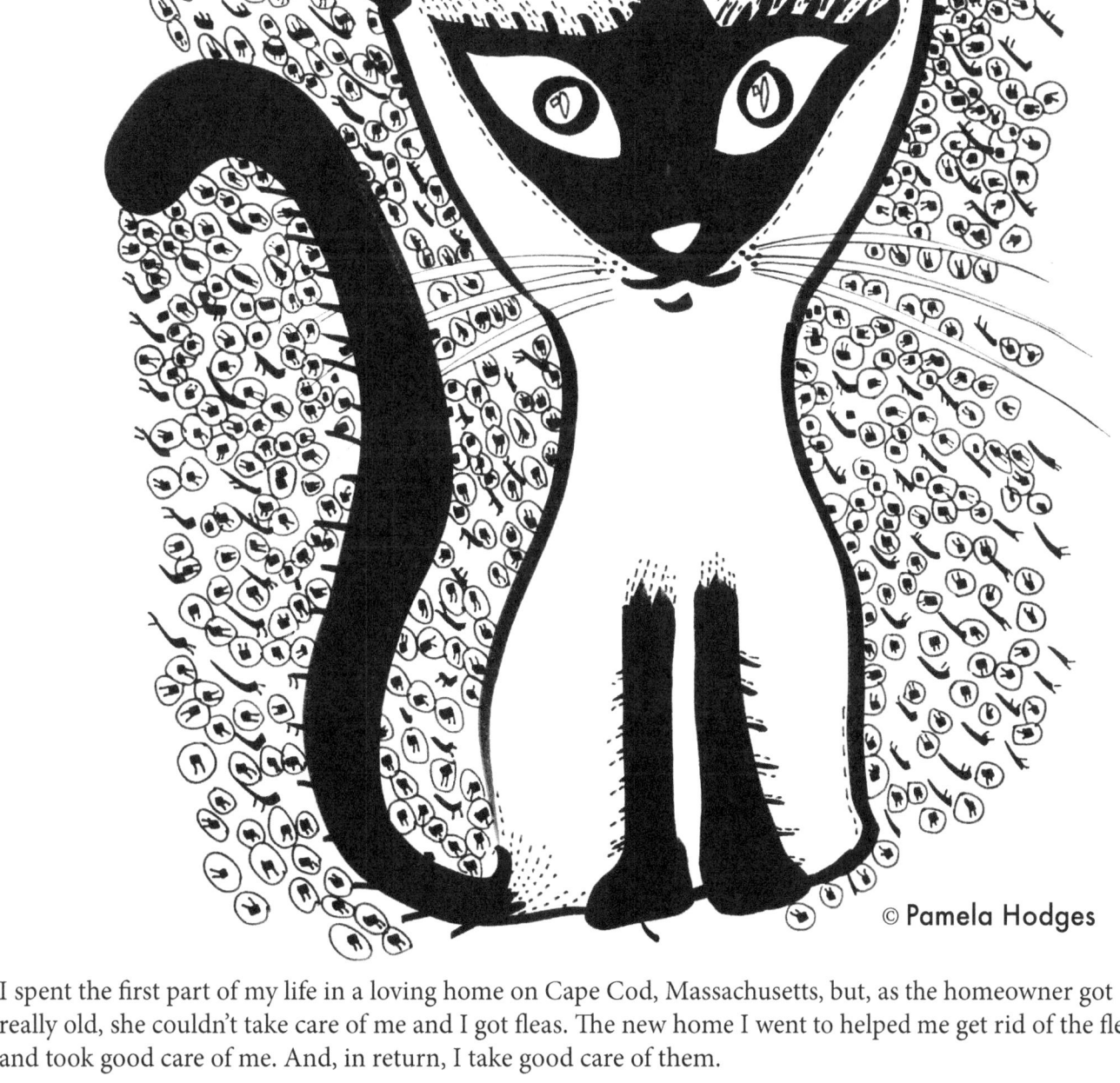

© Pamela Hodges

I spent the first part of my life in a loving home on Cape Cod, Massachusetts, but, as the homeowner got really old, she couldn't take care of me and I got fleas. The new home I went to helped me get rid of the fleas and took good care of me. And, in return, I take good care of them.

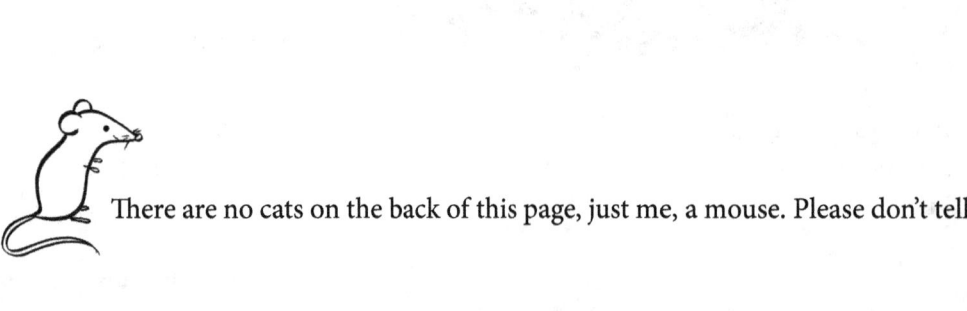
There are no cats on the back of this page, just me, a mouse. Please don't tell the cats I am here.

FLYNN

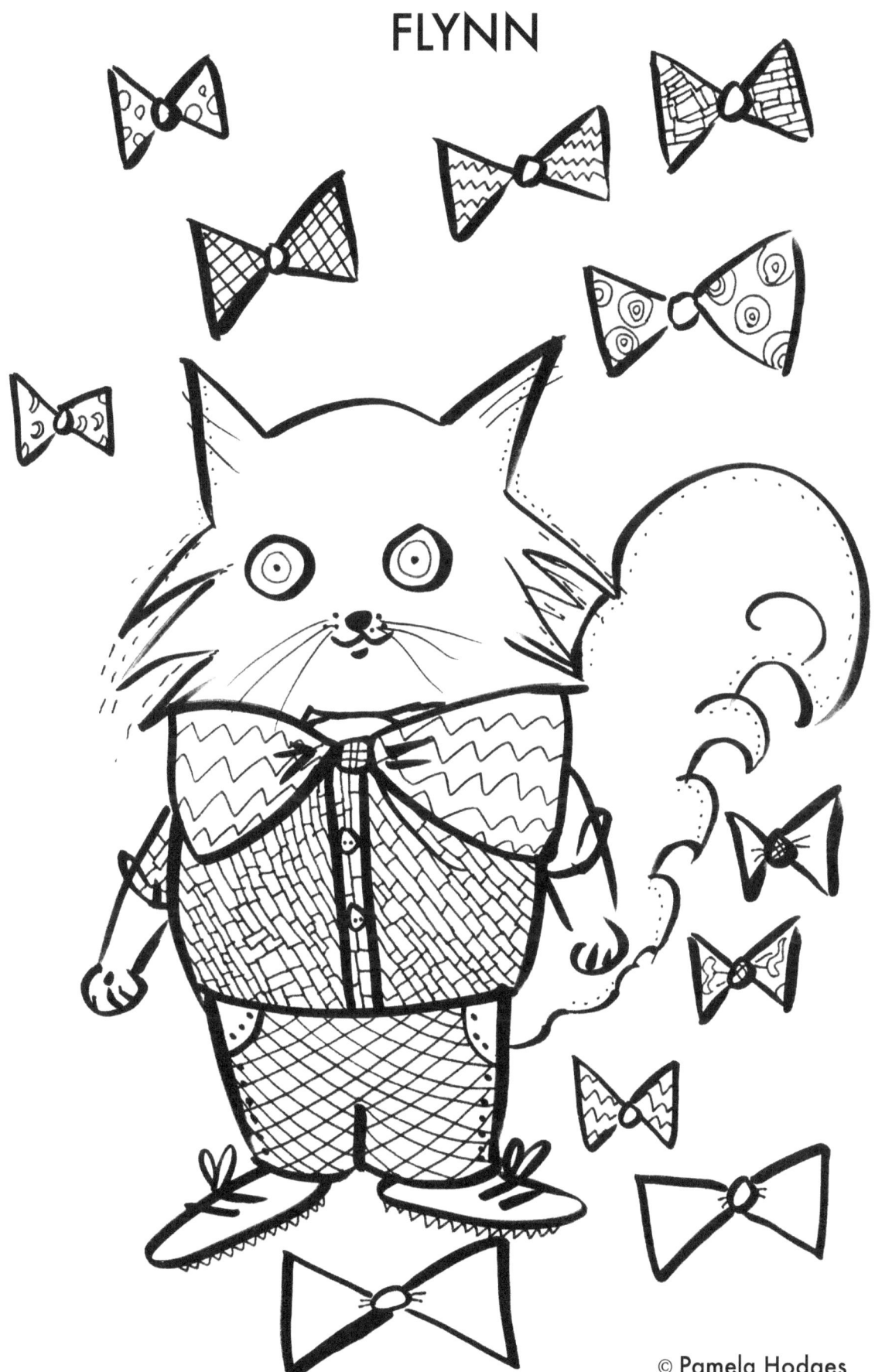

© Pamela Hodges

My brother and I were living outside. A family rescued both of us but really only wanted one cat. When they tried to separate us, I cried and cried and cried until they kept me too. They named me Flynn and my brother Fergus. Crying can help you get what you want.

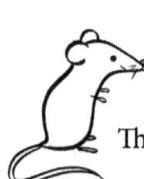 There are no cats on the back of this page, just me, a mouse. Please don't tell the cats I am here.

HARPER

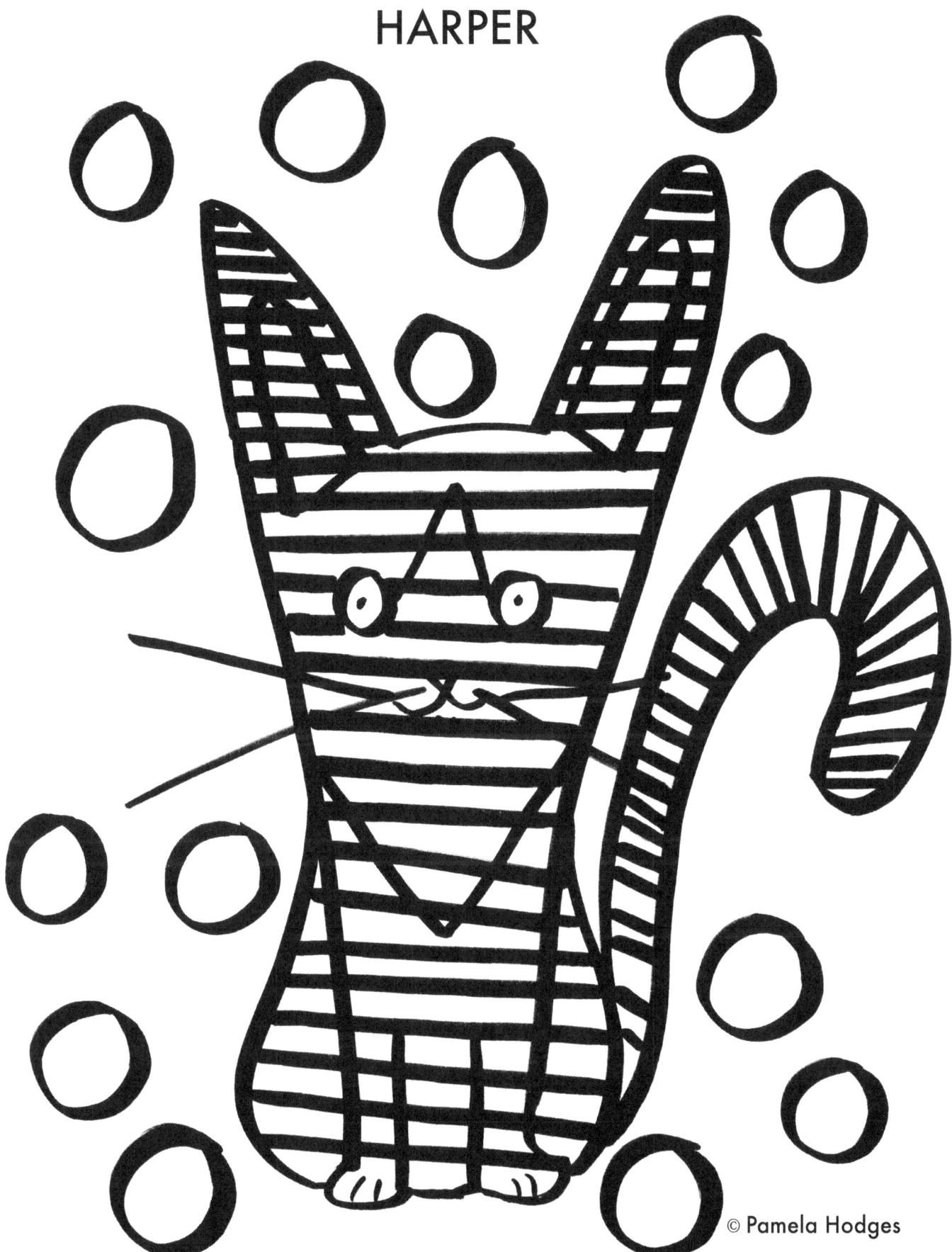

© Pamela Hodges

My typist and rescuer, Pamela Hodges, the same lady who drew all these pictures, named me Harper after the writer Harper Lee. I was born in a barn and abandoned with my brother at an animal rescue in Redding, Pennsylvania. I write at TheCatWhoWrites.com. I am learning how to read. My favorite word is cat.

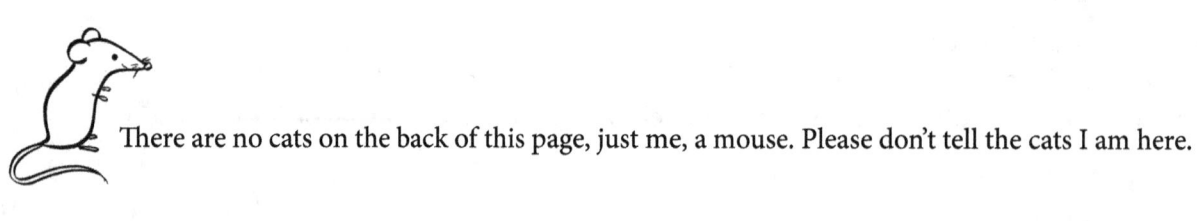 There are no cats on the back of this page, just me, a mouse. Please don't tell the cats I am here.

HARRY TRUMAN

© Pamela Hodges

Supposedly I was a dead ringer for Harry Truman when I was a kitten. I am an Abyssinian cat, red with green eyes. My favorite spot to sit is in the frying pan on the stove (when it is not hot). My nickname is Nid, French for nest.

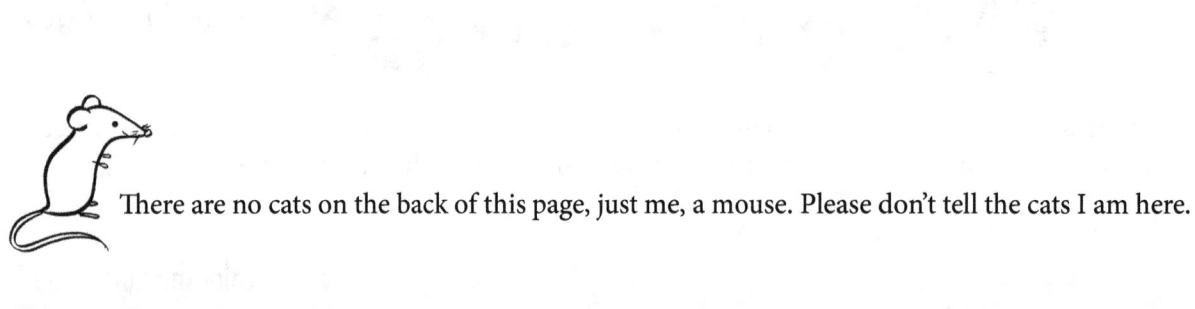 There are no cats on the back of this page, just me, a mouse. Please don't tell the cats I am here.

JAZZ

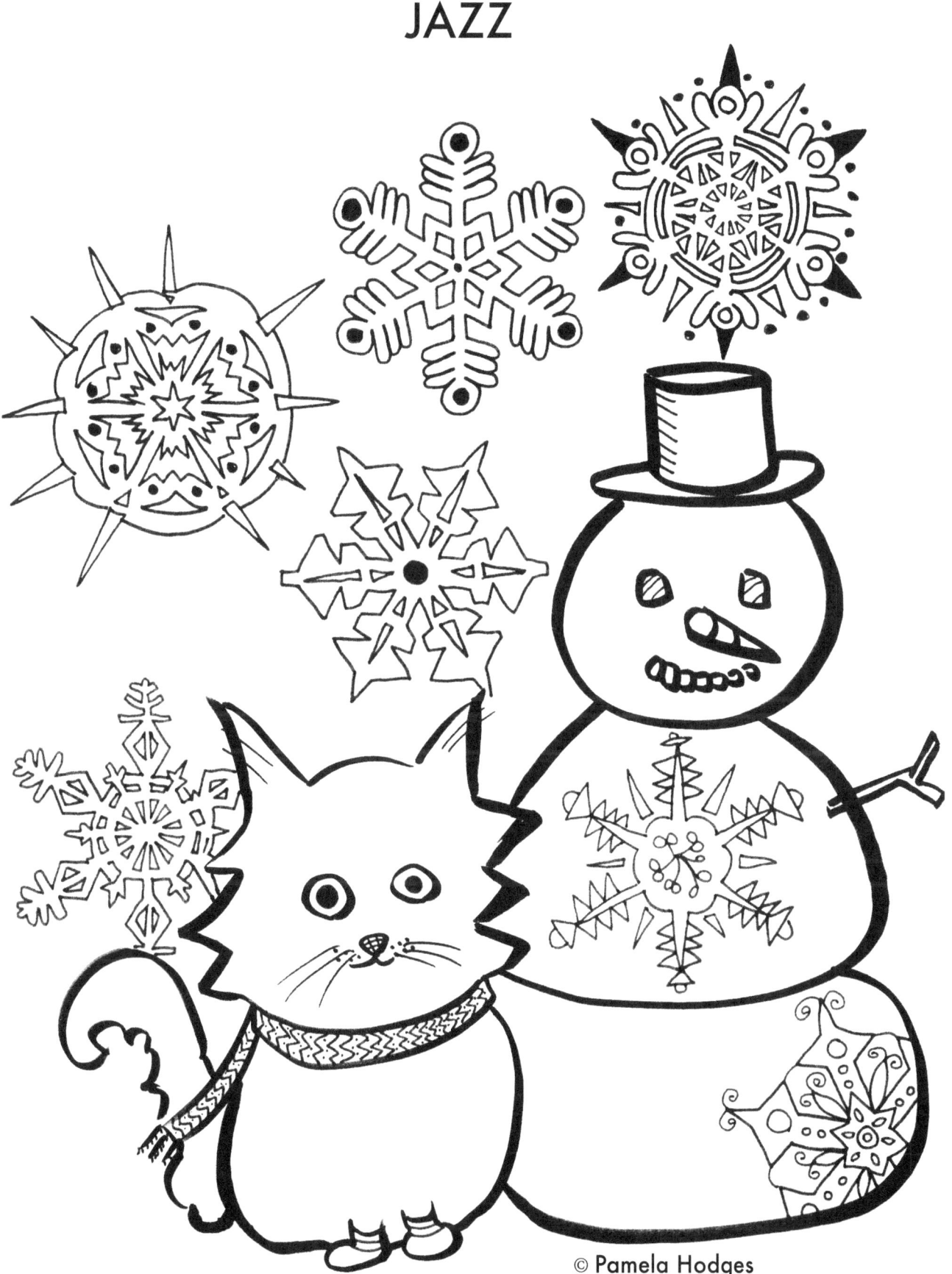

© Pamela Hodges

I was rescued from a snowbank in Saskatoon, Saskatchewan, Canada in February. It was very cold. A little kitten found in the middle of the night in minus thirty-five degree Celsius temperatures. The humans who plucked me from the snow bank saved my life.

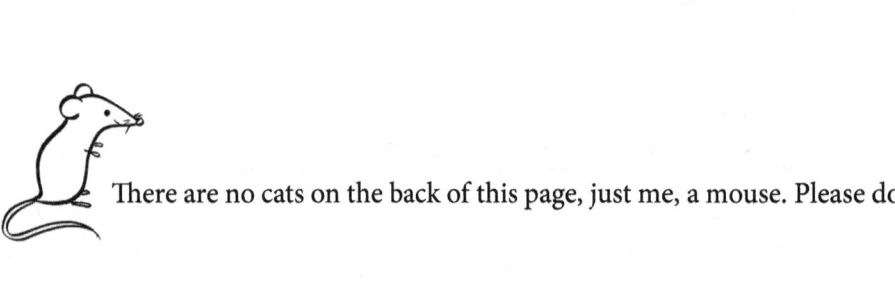There are no cats on the back of this page, just me, a mouse. Please don't tell the cats I am here.

JOI

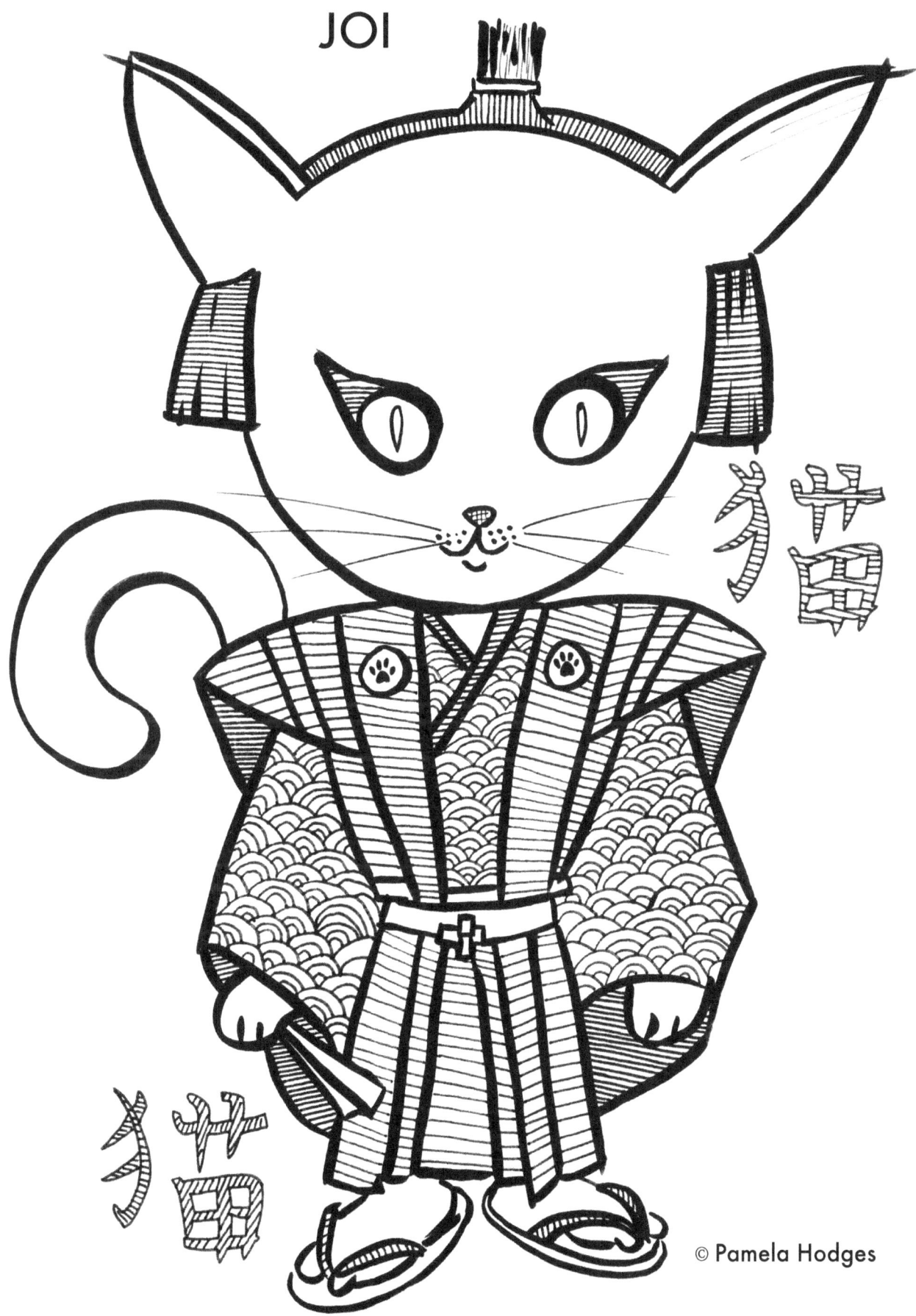

I am Joi. I am from Tokyo, Japan. It is very nice to meet you. I have always wanted to be a samurai warrior, so I was delighted to be drawn as one. The word for cat in Japanese is Neko. Cats say "Nyaa, nyaa," in Japanese, and "Meow, meow," in English.

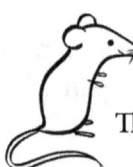 There are no cats on the back of this page, just me, a mouse. Please don't tell the cats I am here.

KANER

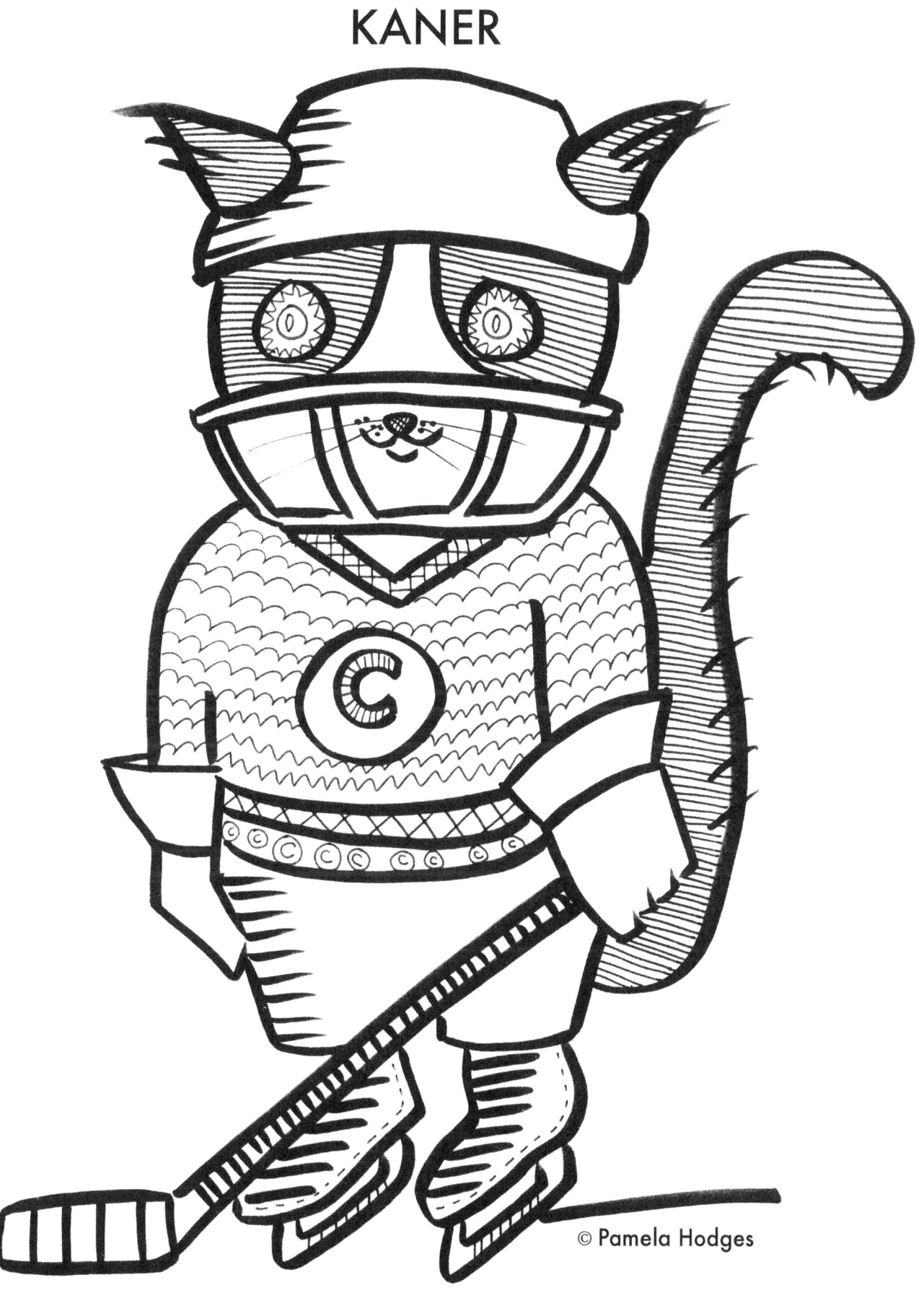

© Pamela Hodges

Hey, I am Kaner. They call me "The Monster Cat." I am at least four feet from top to tail and I weigh in at thirty pounds. I am named after the Blackhawk's Patrick Kane because, when I was a kitten, Patrick Kane had a black eye and we resembled each other.

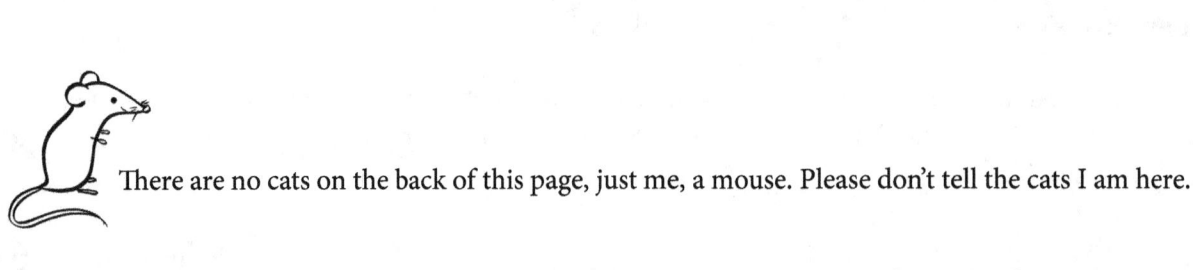

There are no cats on the back of this page, just me, a mouse. Please don't tell the cats I am here.

LARRY

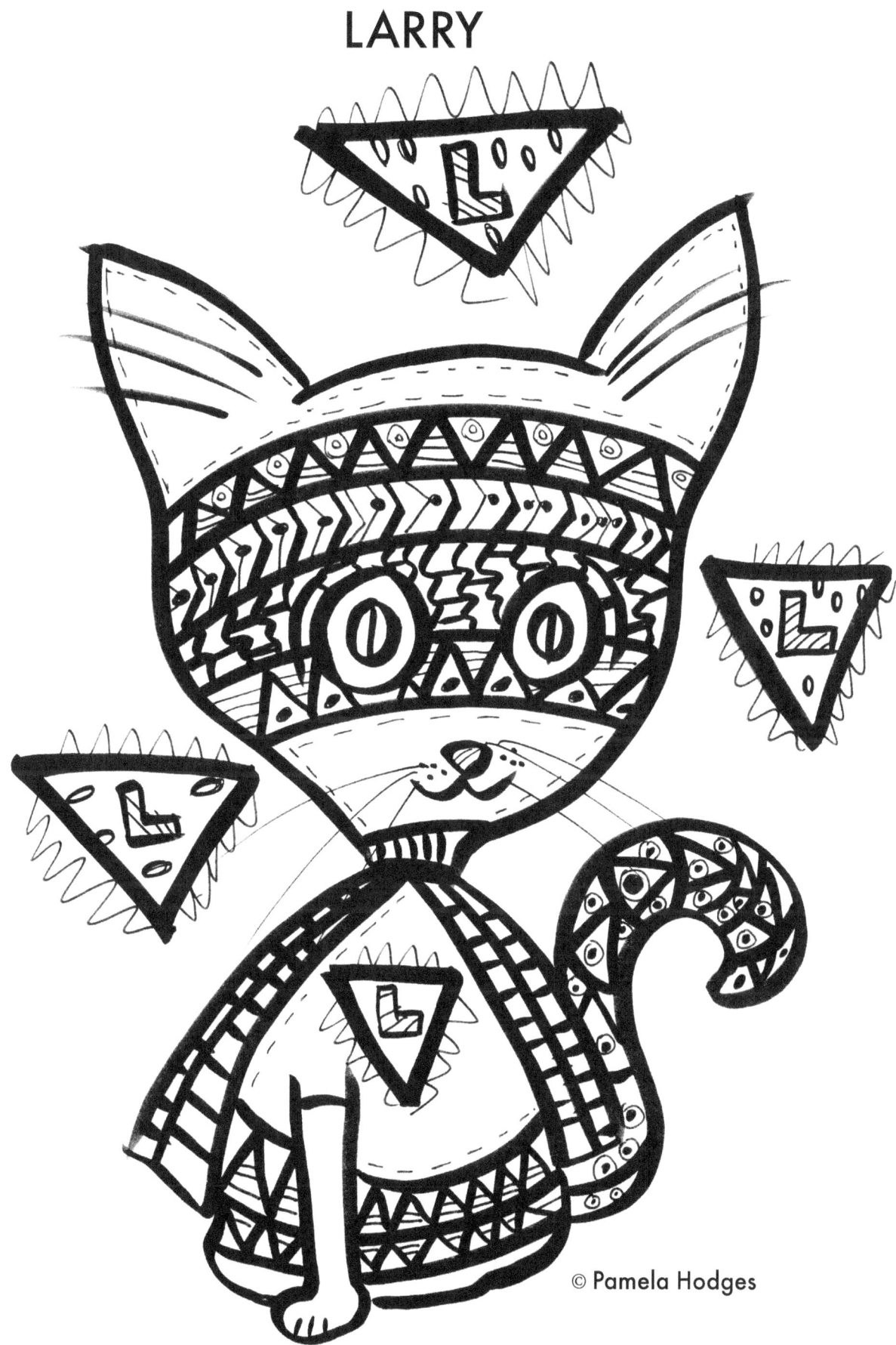

© Pamela Hodges

I was so scared. I was hit by two cars on the highway. A really nice lady ran onto the road and rescued me. She took me to a veterinarian's office. I wear a little vest to help me heal. I don't let my three legs slow me down.

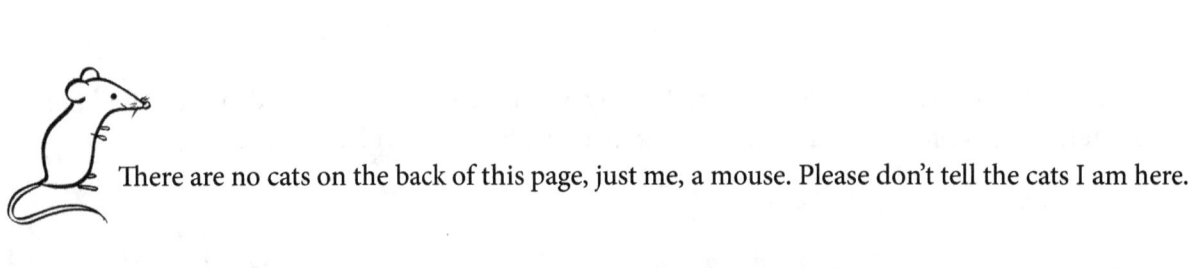 There are no cats on the back of this page, just me, a mouse. Please don't tell the cats I am here.

LATTE

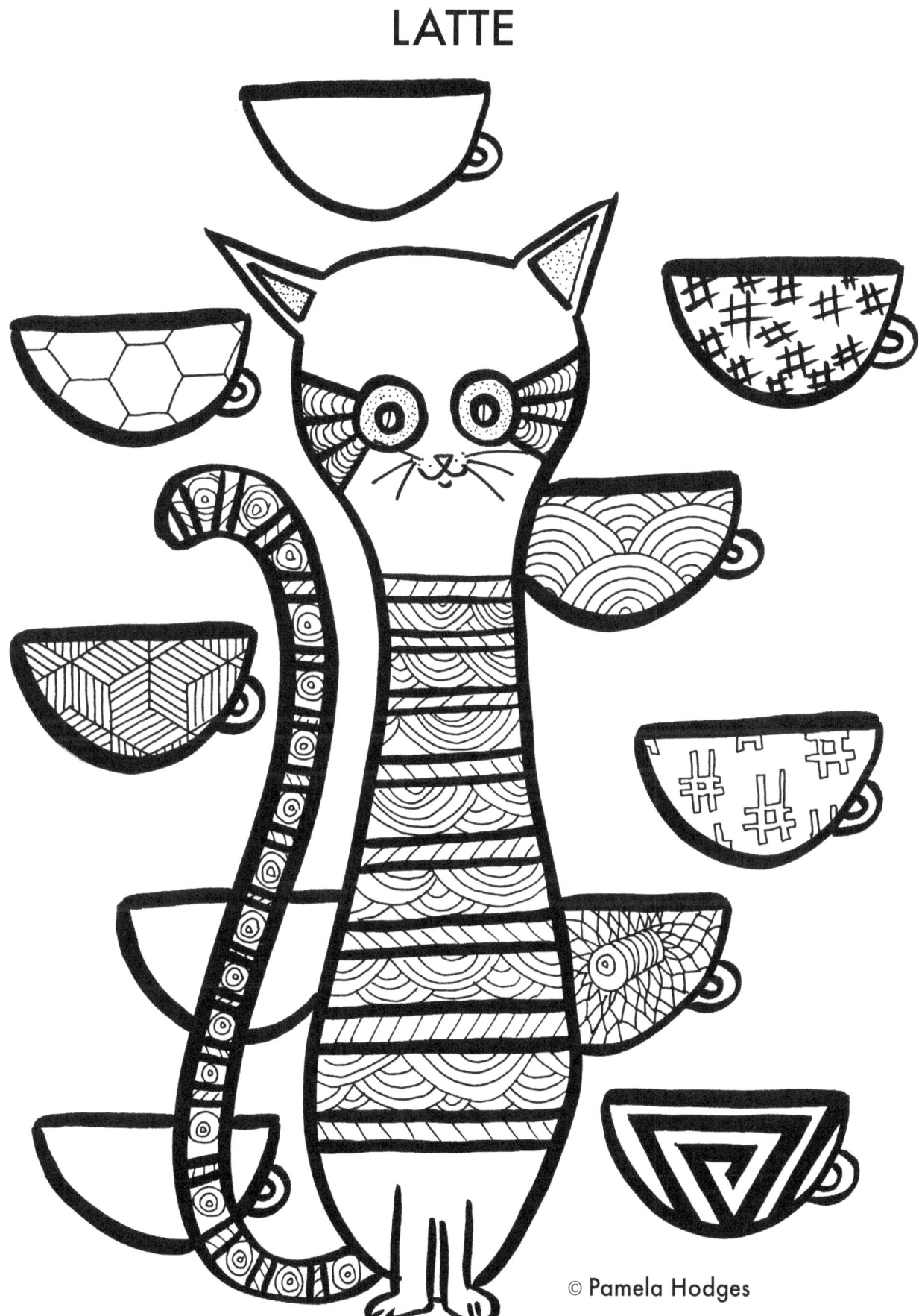

© Pamela Hodges

I was the last kitten to be adopted from a litter of free kittens at a church. No one wanted me because I was long and skinny and I had a long tail, not fat and plump like the other cats. I was offered to a kind woman whose cat had just died. Once I walked through her front door, I felt so much at home, I have never left.

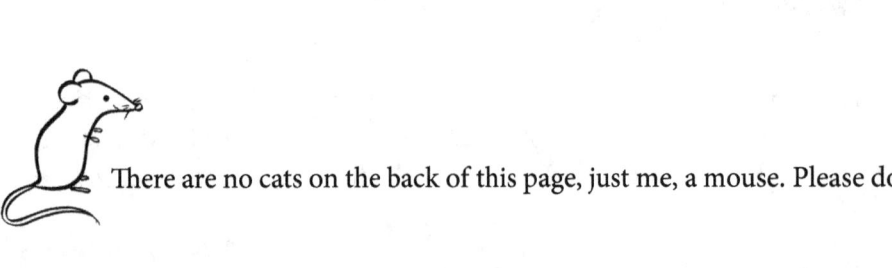
There are no cats on the back of this page, just me, a mouse. Please don't tell the cats I am here.

LILLI

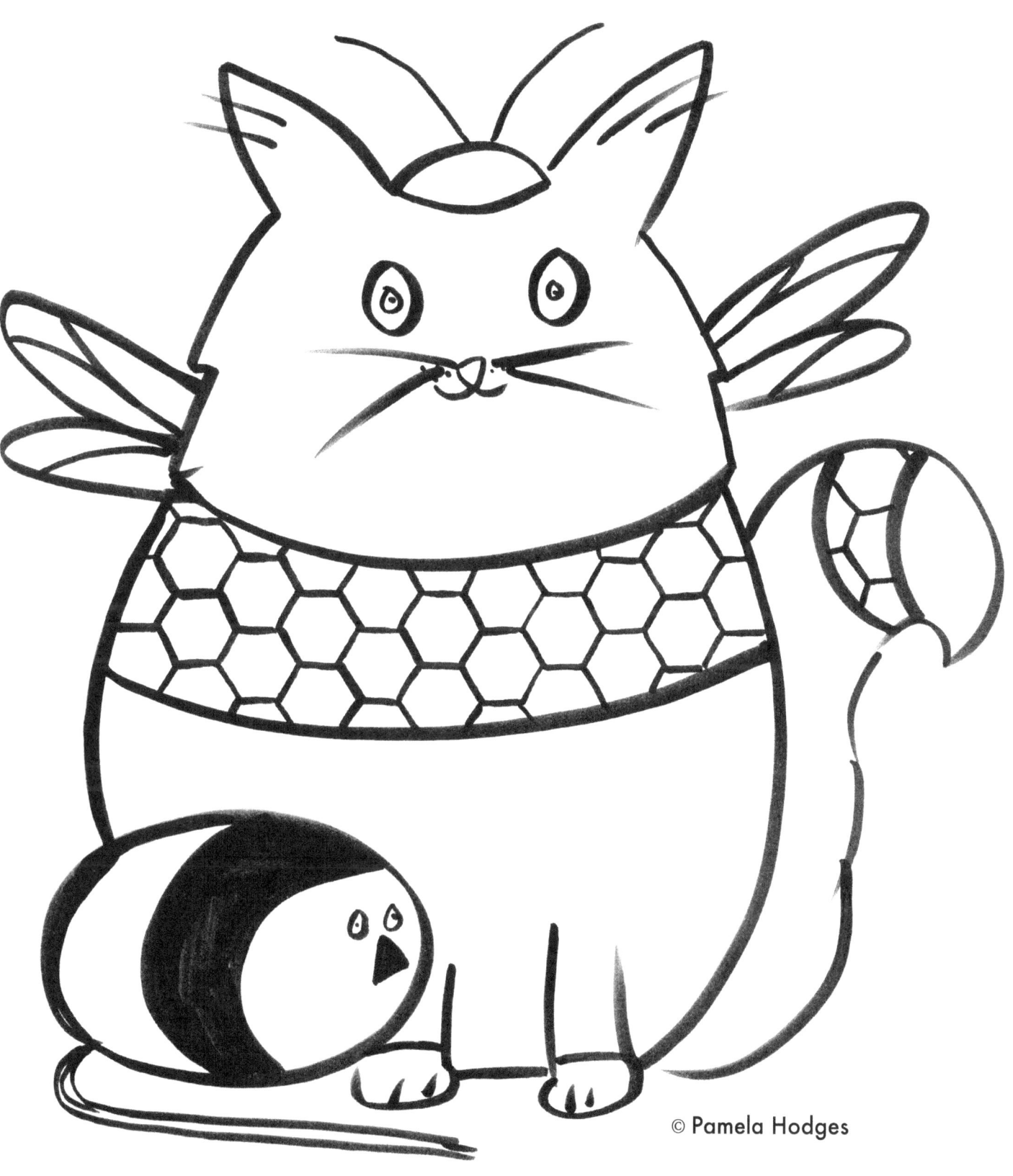

© Pamela Hodges

Hi, my name is Lilli. I was adopted from a pet store. My new mom and dad raced to the store when they got the call that a Chocolate Ragdoll was coming. The store was going to sell me to the first person who paid. I love my new home and my Bumble Bee, Mr. Bumble. I love my humans. I am glad they got there first.

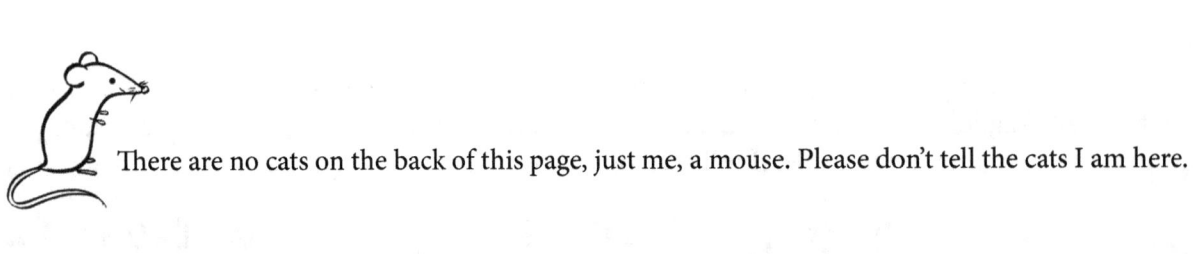 There are no cats on the back of this page, just me, a mouse. Please don't tell the cats I am here.

LITTLE BIT

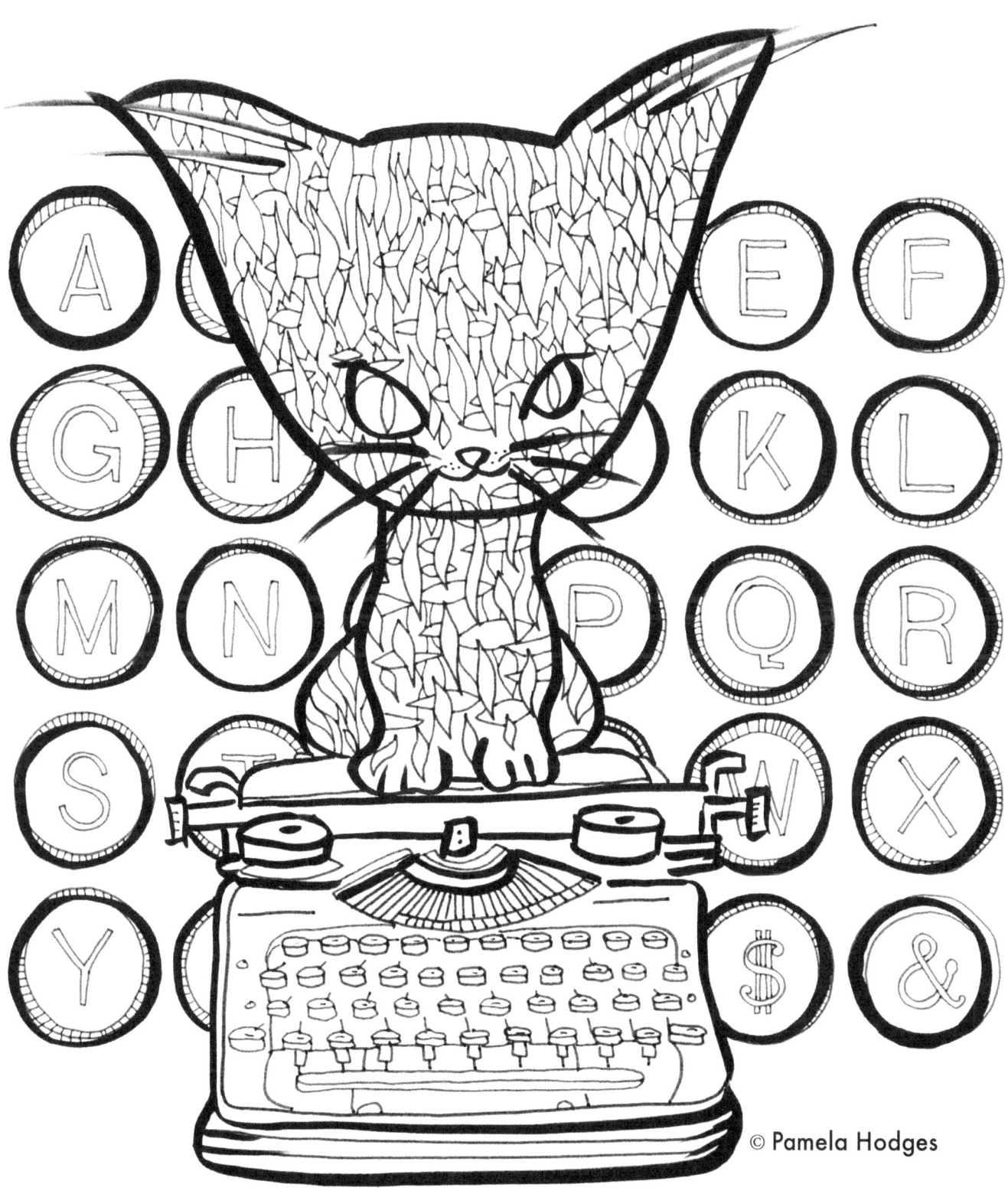

© Pamela Hodges

I am Little Bit. I wandered into a fenced backyard after being dumped in a back alley with my mommy and brothers and sisters. A dog who lived there grabbed me in her mouth. After an emergency trip to the veterinarian, the family adopted me. They said I was very brave.

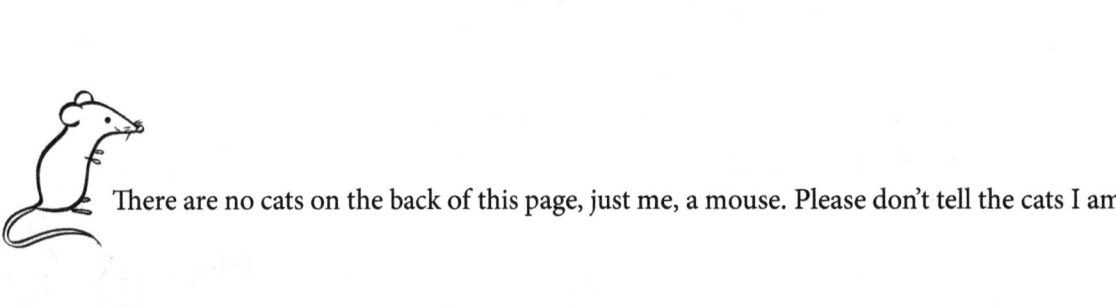 There are no cats on the back of this page, just me, a mouse. Please don't tell the cats I am here.

LYRA

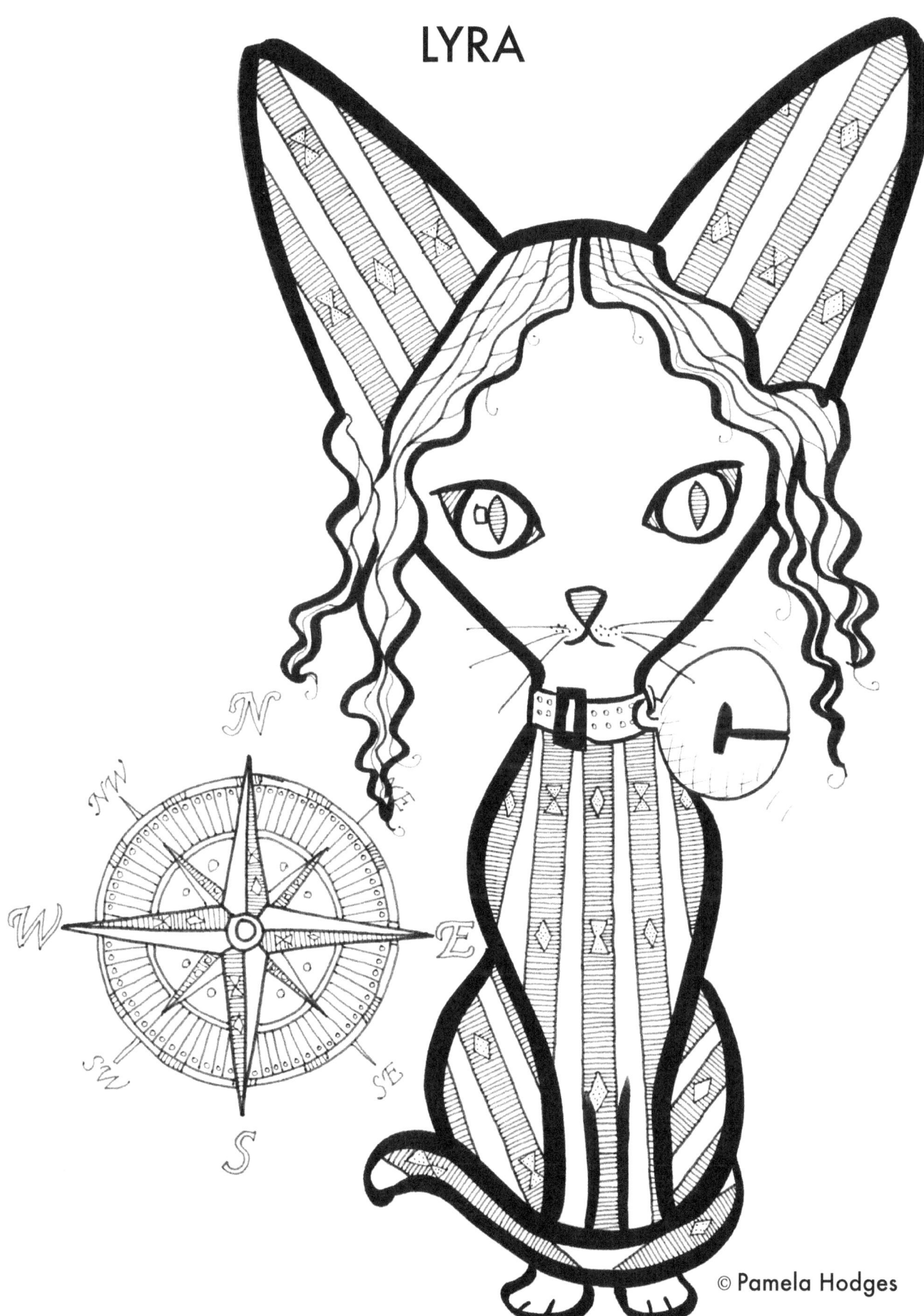

© Pamela Hodges

I was rescued from the busy C5 Highway in Manila, Philippines. My mother named me Lyra Belazquia after a character in her favorite book, The Golden Compass. I love to hunt and I am very adventurous. P. S. Will you please tell my mother that I hate my collar?

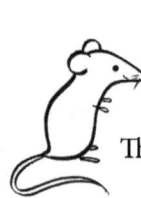 There are no cats on the back of this page, just me, a mouse. Please don't tell the cats I am here.

MACKAYLA

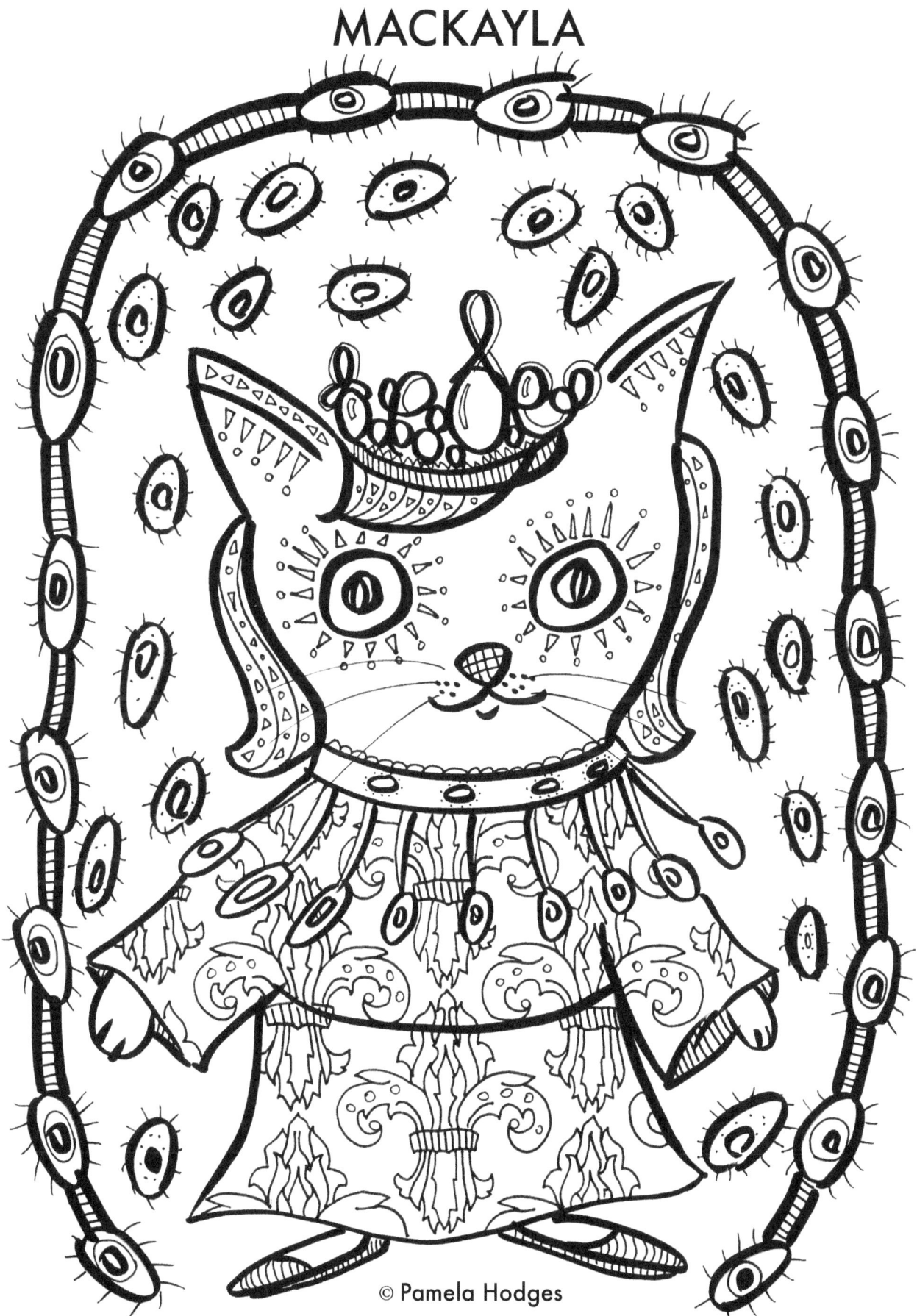

© Pamela Hodges

I was a tiny, tiny, tiny, kitten meowing as loud as I could from under a car parked on the street. It was raining and a cold, nasty evening. I could see feet walking past me. They heard me and brought me home! Now I manage the house for them.

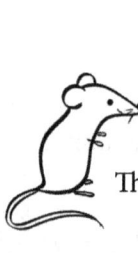There are no cats on the back of this page, just me, a mouse. Please don't tell the cats I am here.

MILO

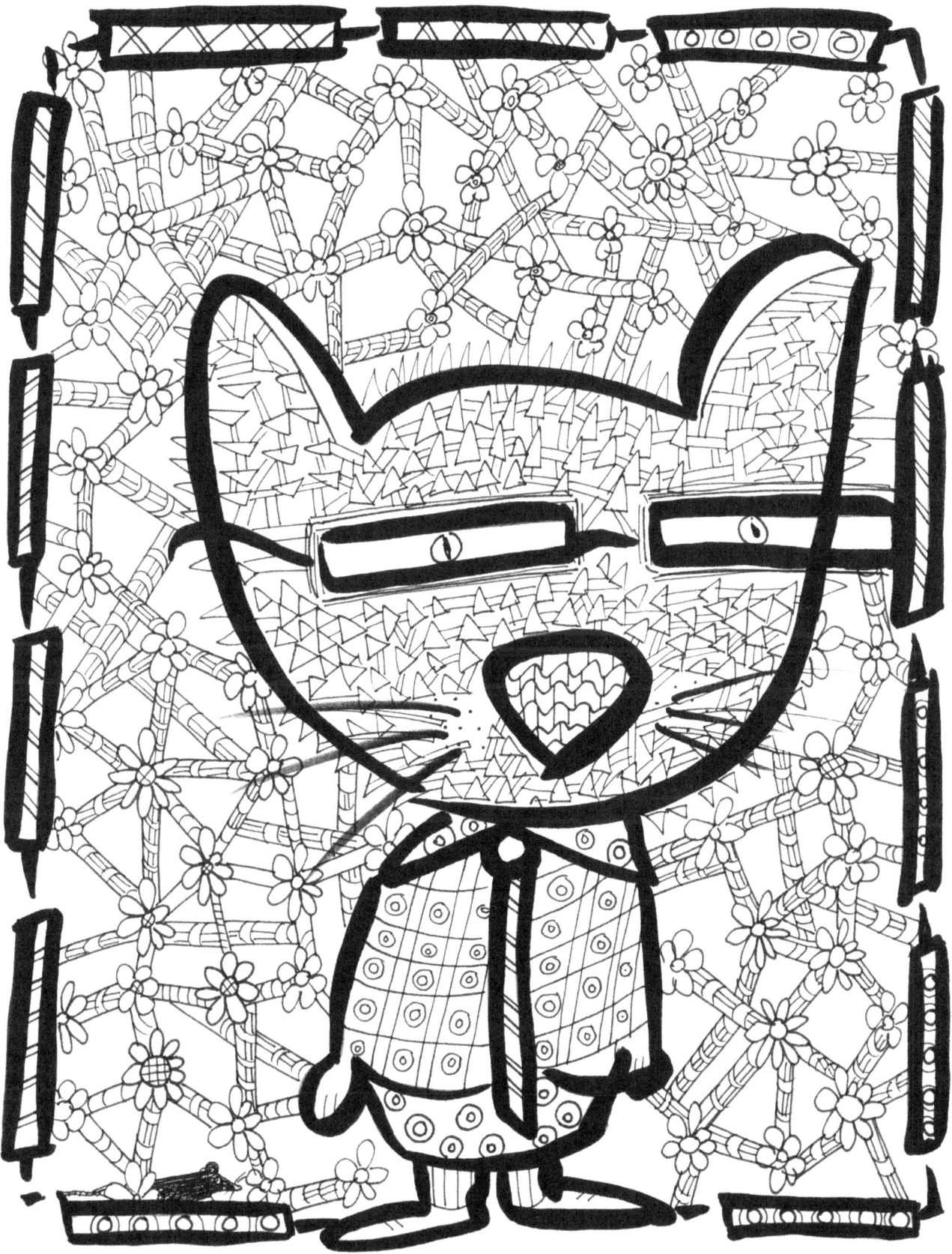

I am sort of a rescue cat. My mommy's daughter was at Walmart one day and saw a lady with a box of kittens. She saw me and took me to my new home. I am not sure what would have happened to me if I was not rescued from the parking lot. Oh, I am Milo.

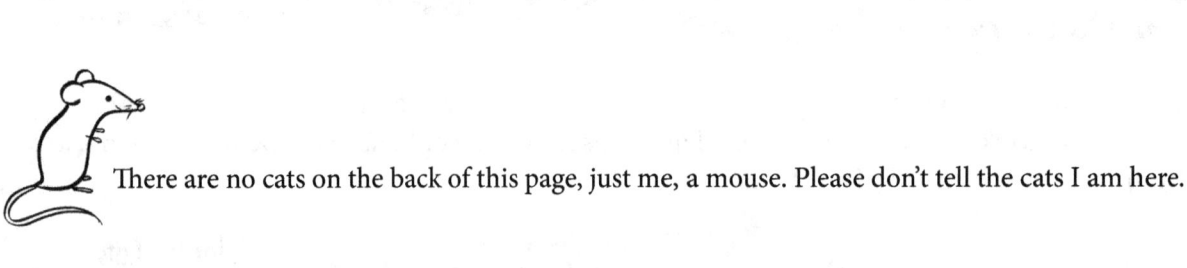 There are no cats on the back of this page, just me, a mouse. Please don't tell the cats I am here.

MIMI

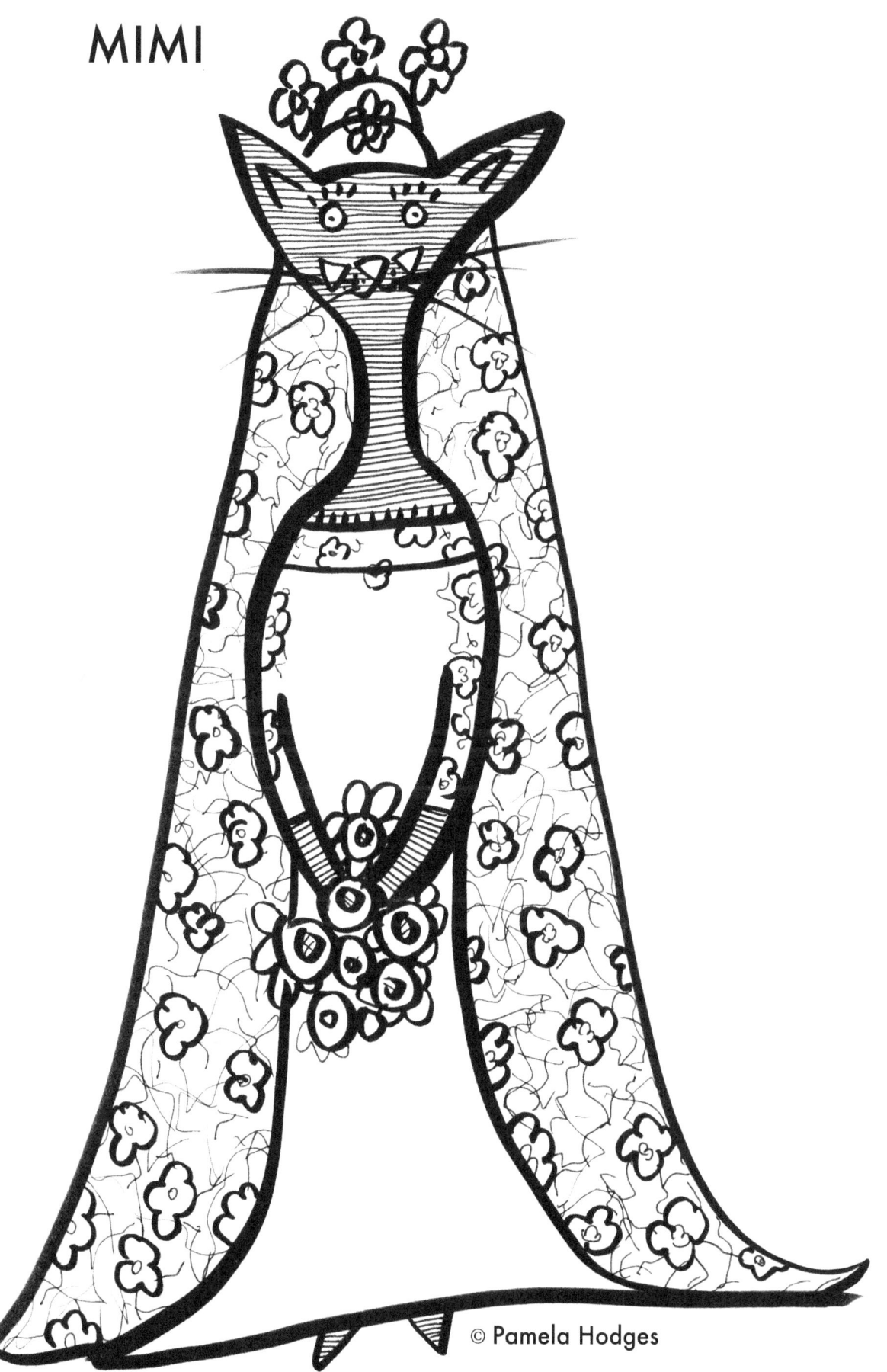

© Pamela Hodges

I am Mimi, French for Mignon Simon. I was given to a teacher three years ago by her supervisor. I was taken down from a tree during a horrible rainstorm, in Louisiana. I am not an outside cat, but I do love to climb the Christmas tree every year. Perhaps one year I will go to France; I would love to visit Zoe.

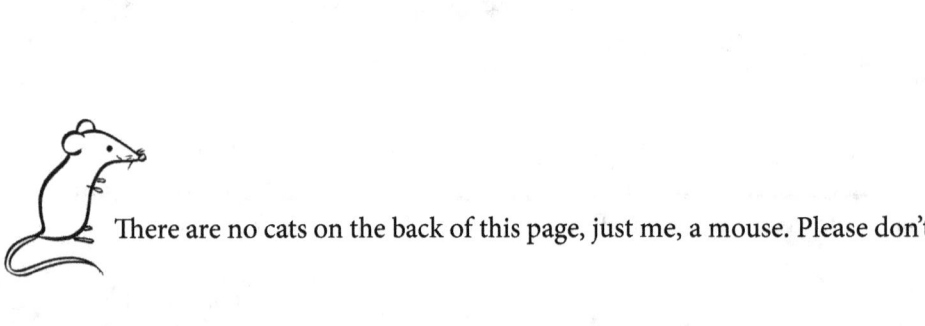 There are no cats on the back of this page, just me, a mouse. Please don't tell the cats I am here.

MOKKA

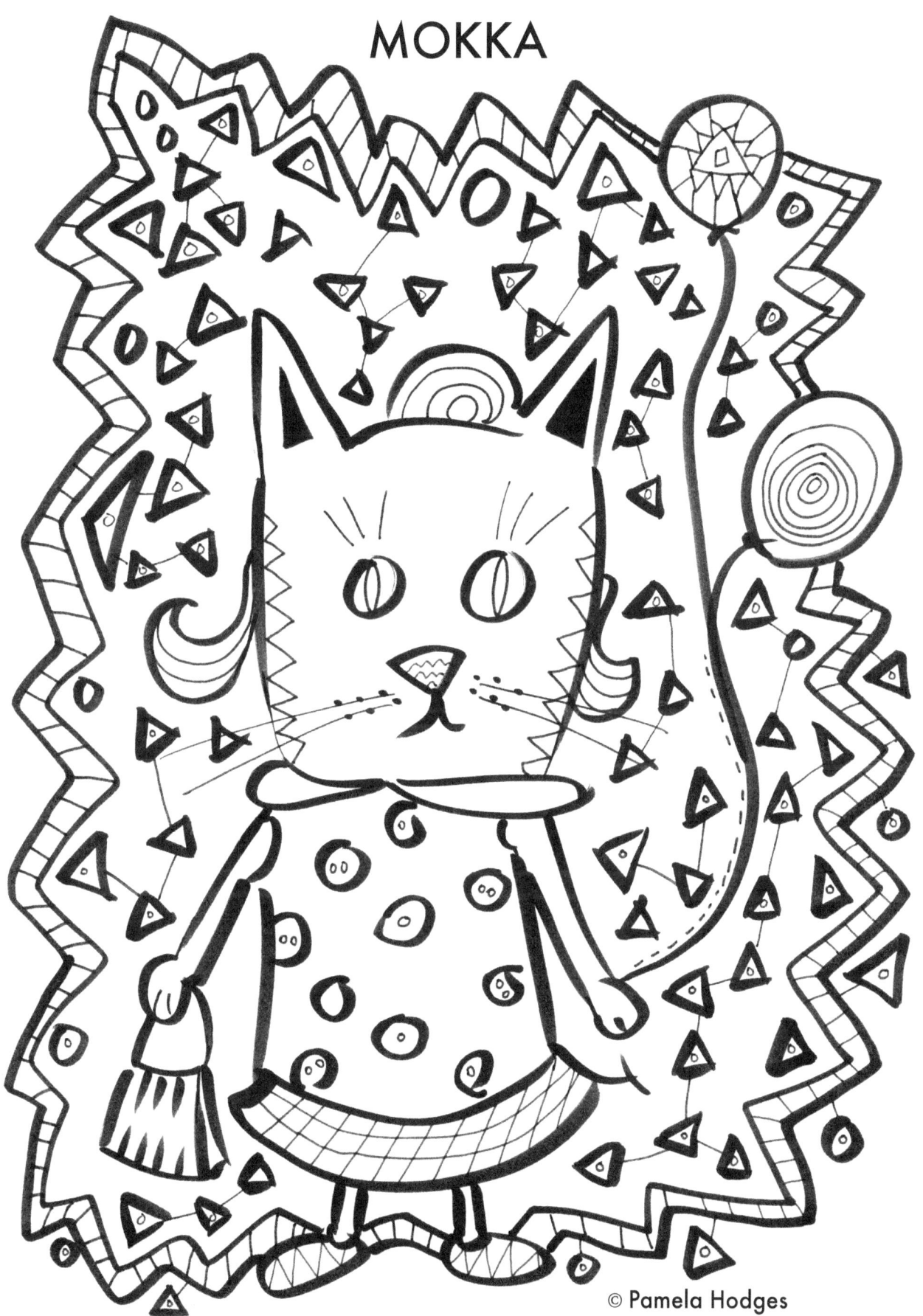

© Pamela Hodges

My name is Mokka and I live in Denmark. I was rescued from a cat hoarder's home. The cat hoarder lady had nineteen cats and couldn't take care of all of us. I love my new home and the little girl who takes care of me.

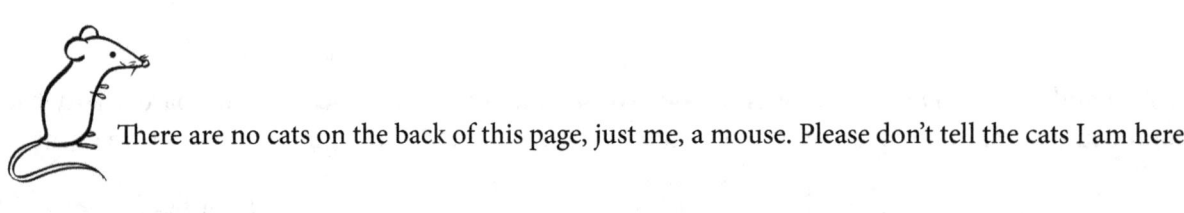 There are no cats on the back of this page, just me, a mouse. Please don't tell the cats I am here.

PATRICIA

© Pamela Hodges

My name is Patricia. I love to sail and eat ice-cream before my dinner. I was rescued from a boring life of living off the land, and now I sail around the world on my sailboat, Mojito, with James, another cool cat from South Africa.

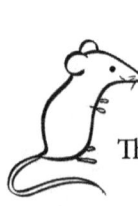There are no cats on the back of this page, just me, a mouse. Please don't tell the cats I am here.

RUPI

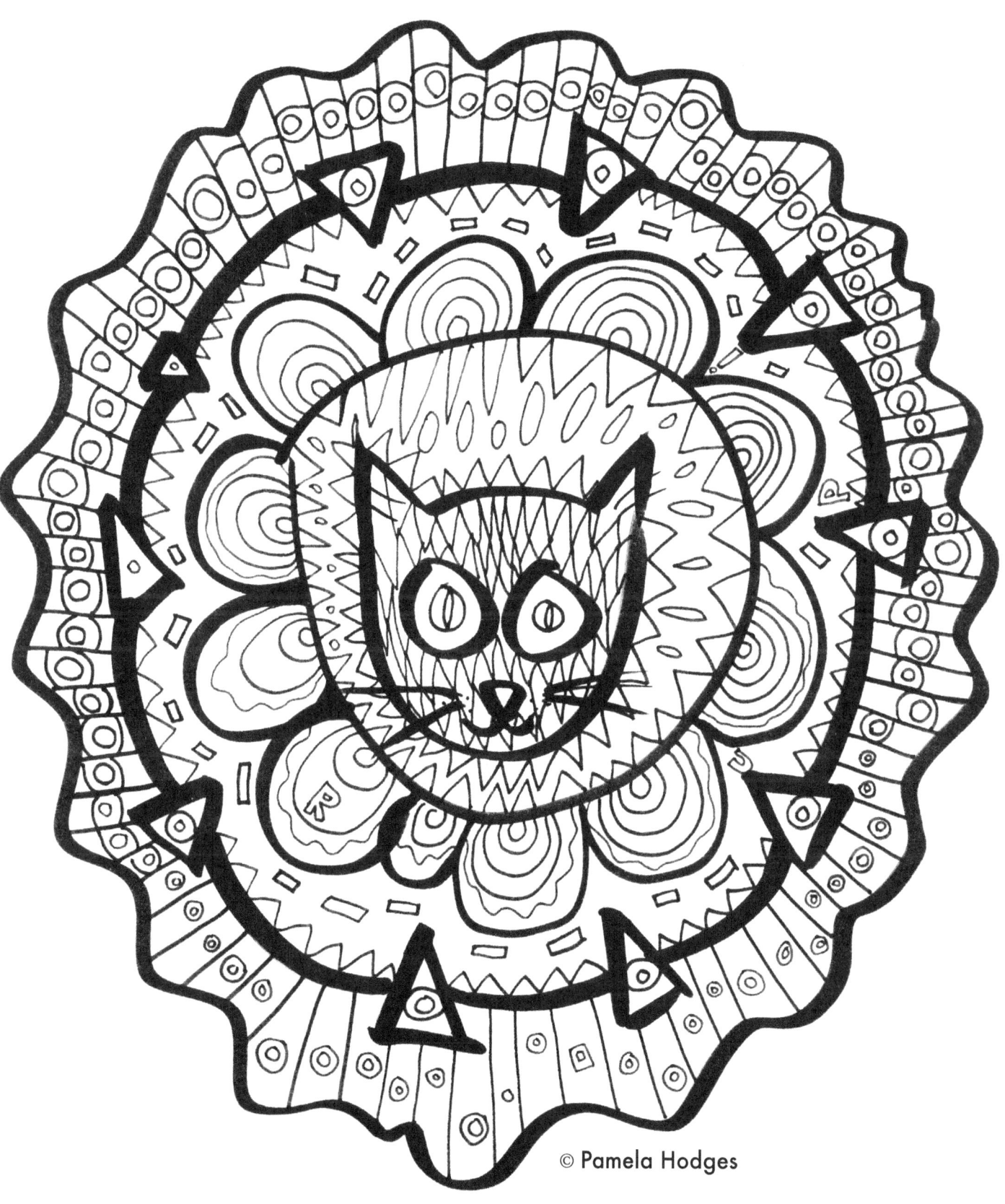

© Pamela Hodges

I was just a little ball of black fluff when I was adopted from the animal shelter in Calgary, Alberta, Canada. My human mother was going to adopt an older cat, but as soon as her friend placed me in her hand, I climbed up her arm and wrapped myself around her neck. She fell in love with me and took me home.

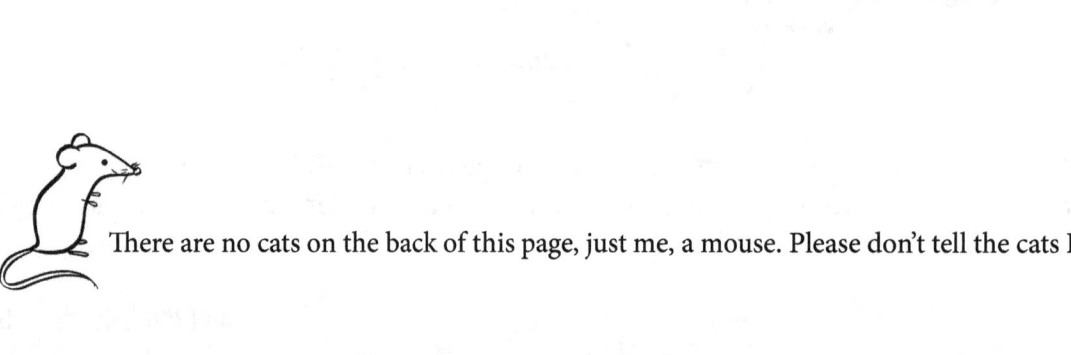 There are no cats on the back of this page, just me, a mouse. Please don't tell the cats I am here.

SASSY

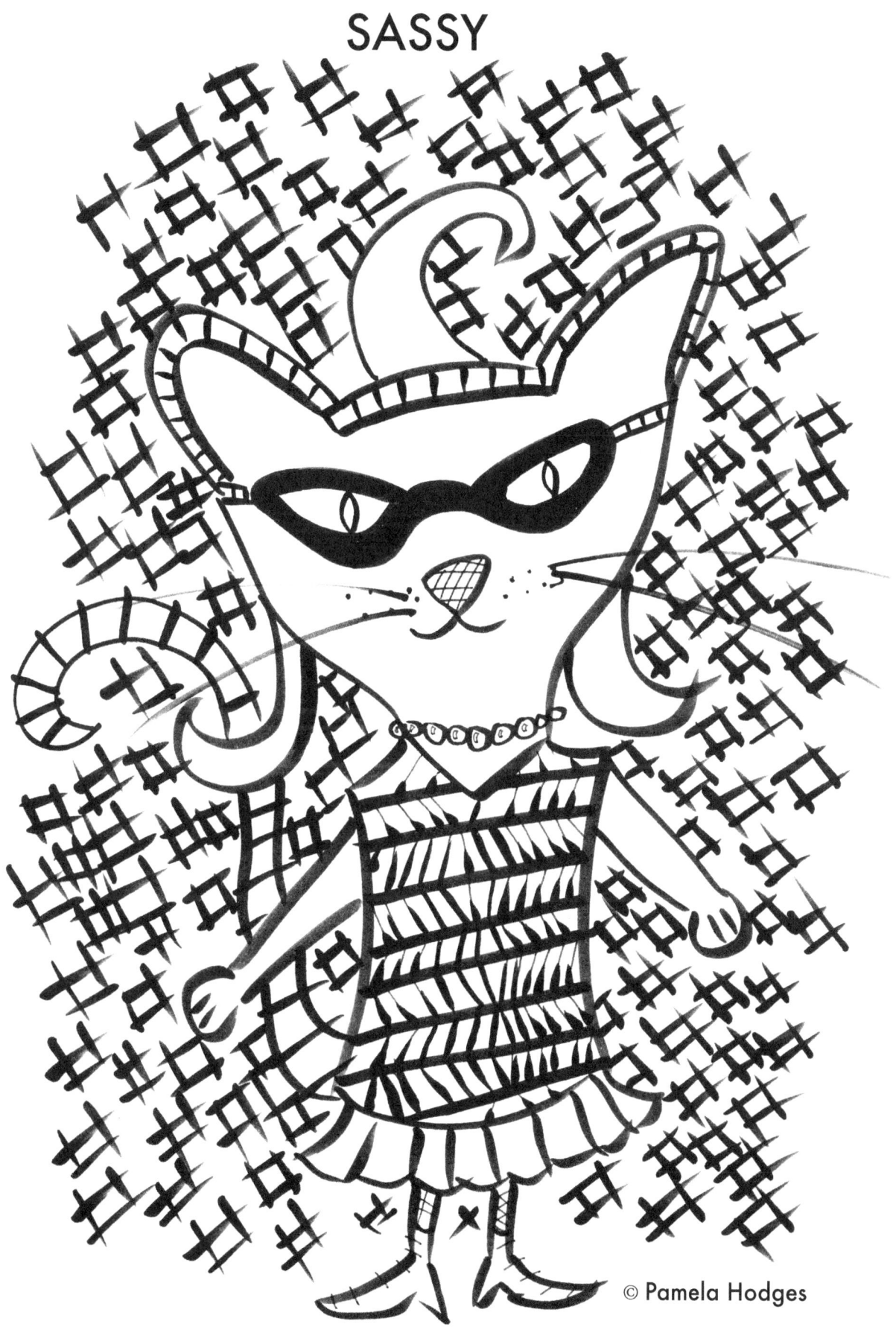

© Pamela Hodges

When I'm not busy assisting with blogging or book writing, I move my toys into interesting patterns to see if my guardians can figure out the message. I live on a farm and I love it here. I wonder why they called me Sassy? I am not Sassy; I am sweet and kind.

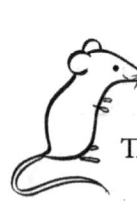 There are no cats on the back of this page, just me, a mouse. Please don't tell the cats I am here.

SKITTLES

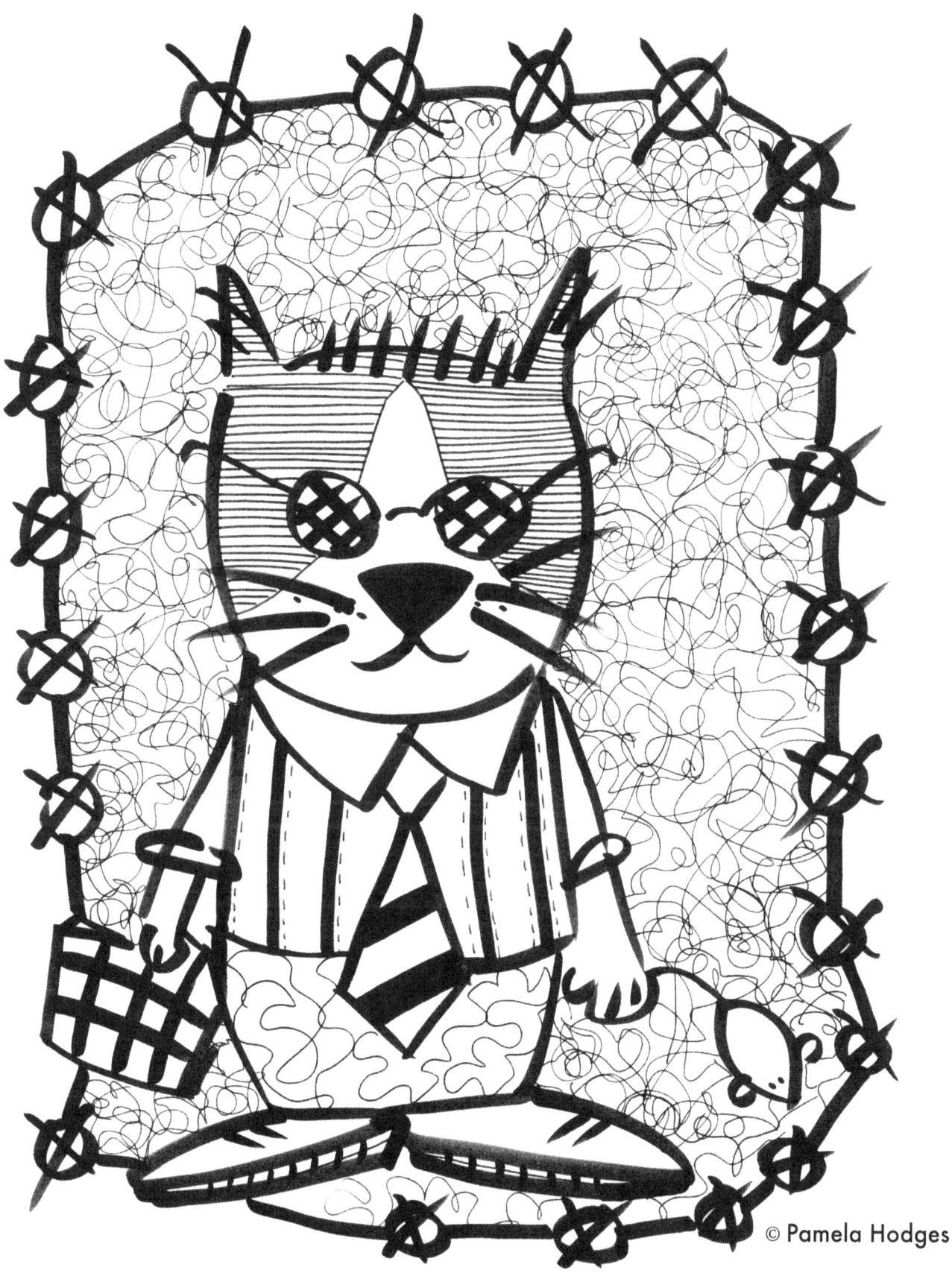

© Pamela Hodges

In the early spring, I was a wild kitten living outside with other feral cats. Then a nice lady caught me and had me fixed through a TNR (trap, neuter, release) program. I was very friendly so she gave me to a nice family where I manage the household. They named me Skittles.

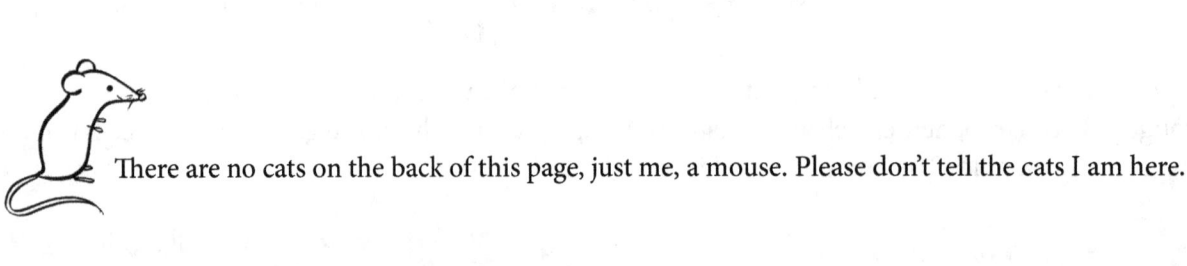 There are no cats on the back of this page, just me, a mouse. Please don't tell the cats I am here.

SMOKEY

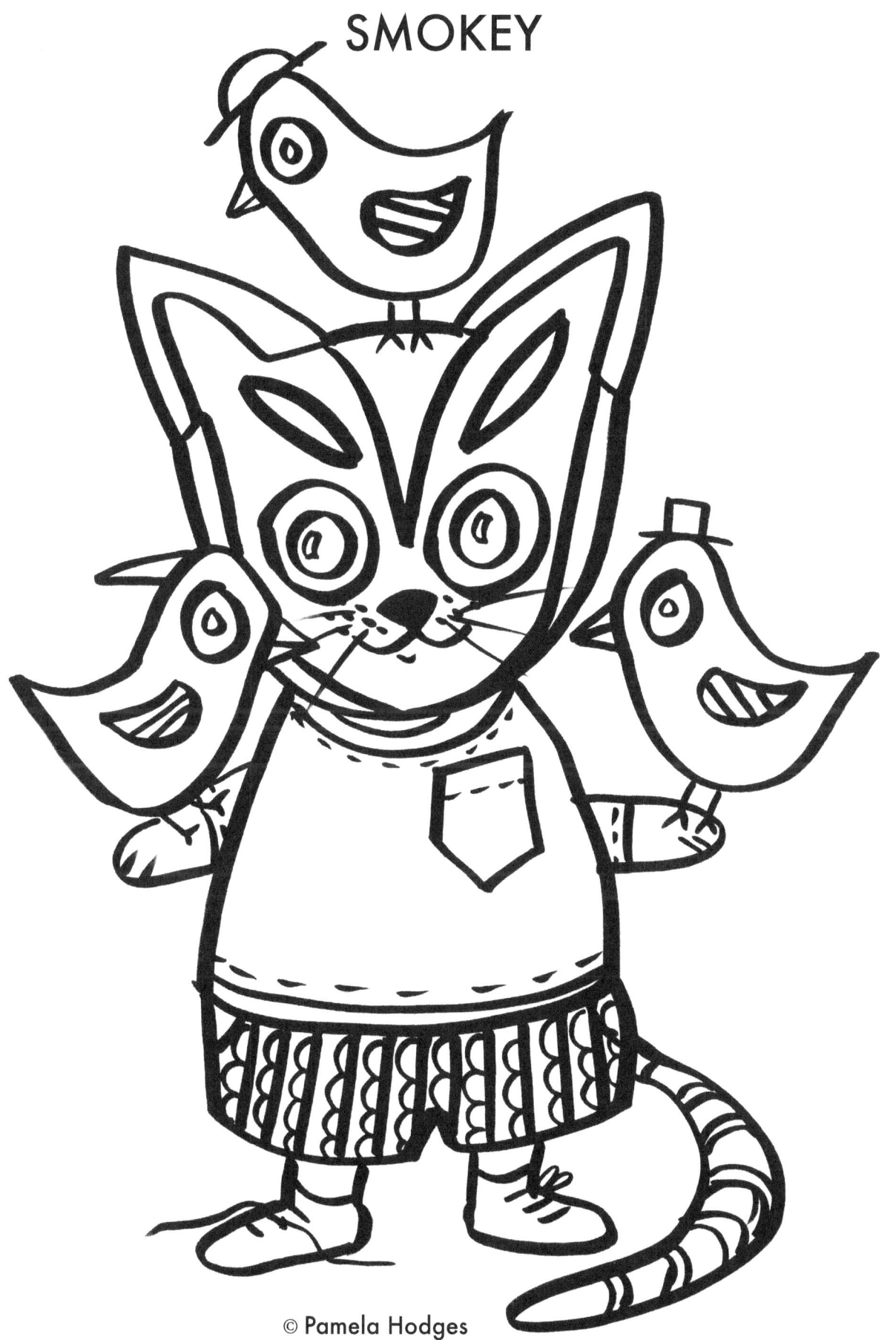

© Pamela Hodges

I was adopted from a cat rescue that had hundreds of cats. The family fell in love with me and my brother, Toby. They put together something called the Smokey and Toby fund and each person in the family contributed money to rescue us. I am Smokey and I like to watch birds.

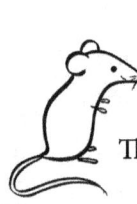 There are no cats on the back of this page, just me, a mouse. Please don't tell the cats I am here.

SPOCK

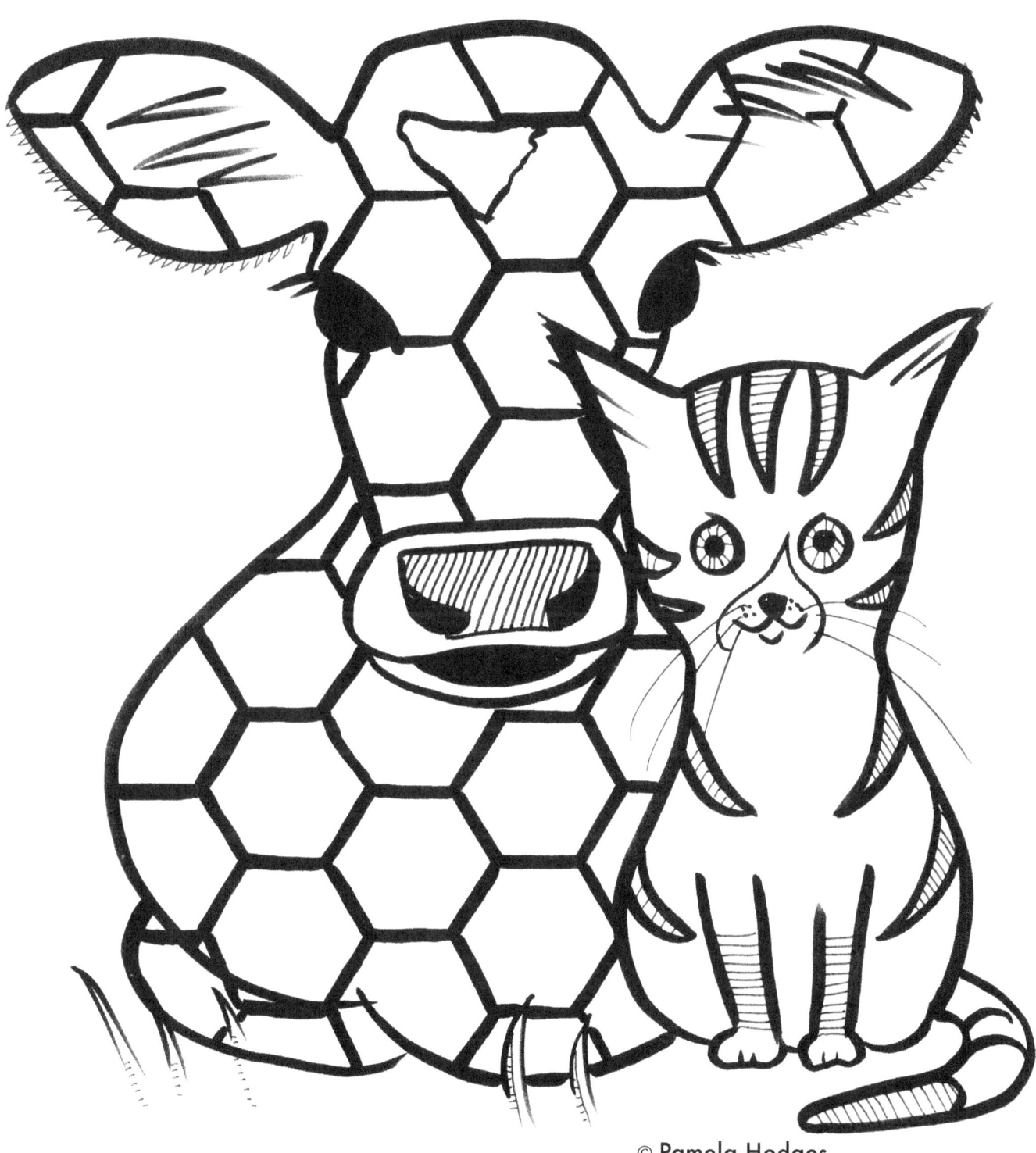

© Pamela Hodges

My cat mother abandoned me at the dairy farm in Australia where I was born. But the artist, Kath, who lives on the farm, took me in and fed me. I rode under the hood of a car for six hours all the way to Sydney once. I am an adventurer just like my namesake, Spock.

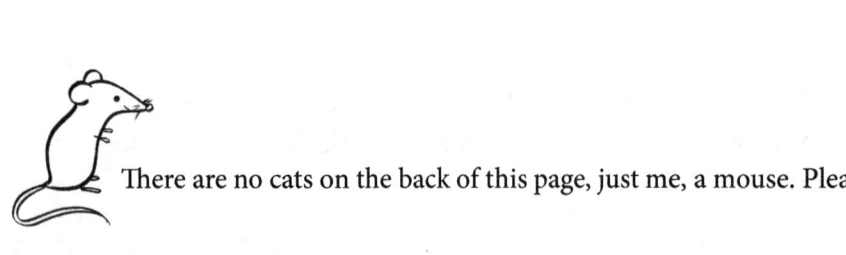There are no cats on the back of this page, just me, a mouse. Please don't tell the cats I am here.

TARDIS

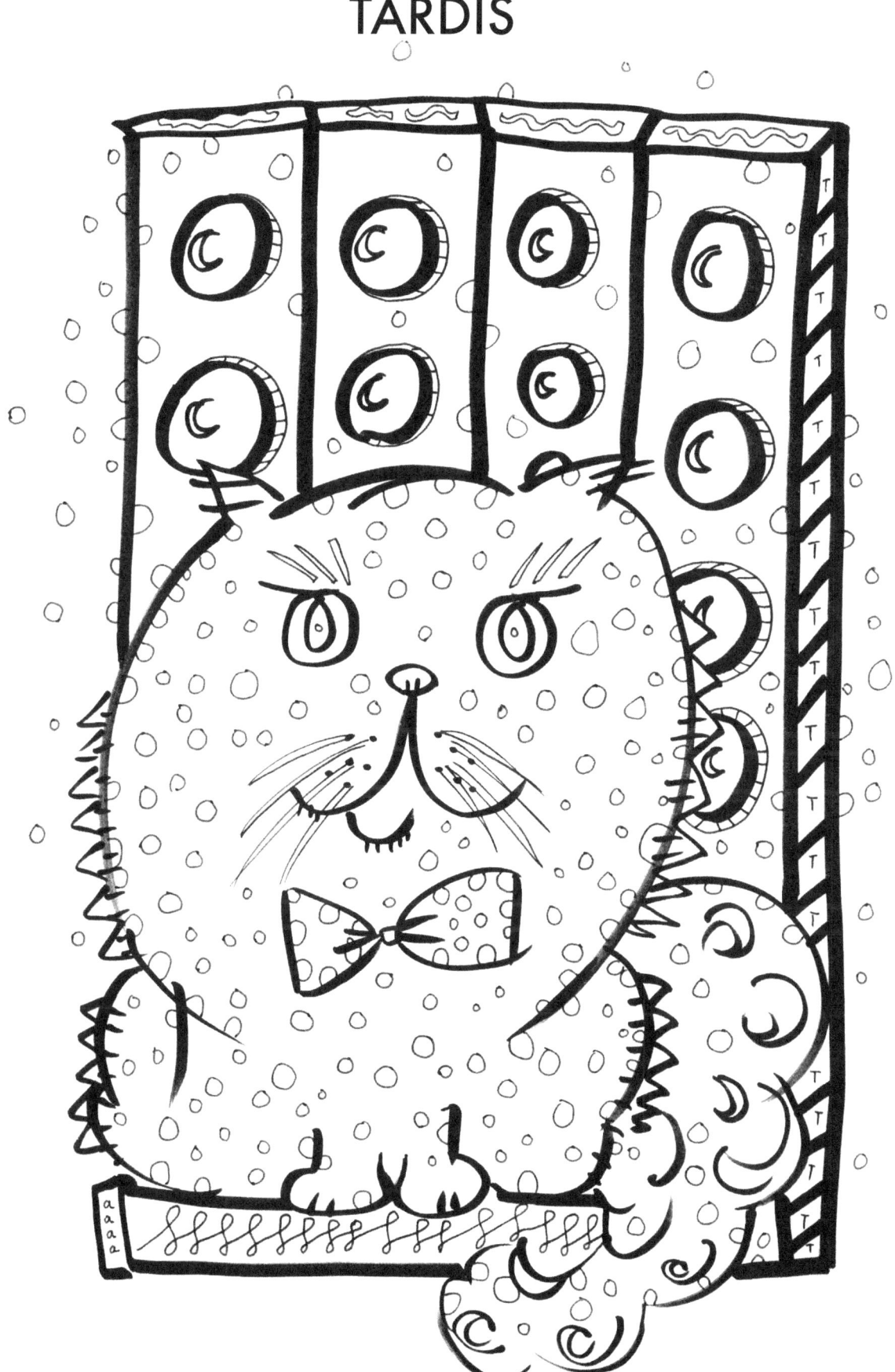

I live with my mom, but I go to Grandma's house a lot because Mom works. But I don't mind because Grandma has better food. I like to jump on the table tardi eat people food, but they keep pushing me off. I don't understand why.

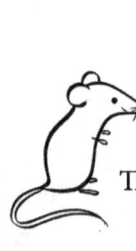 There are no cats on the back of this page, just me, a mouse. Please don't tell the cats I am here.

THE BEAST

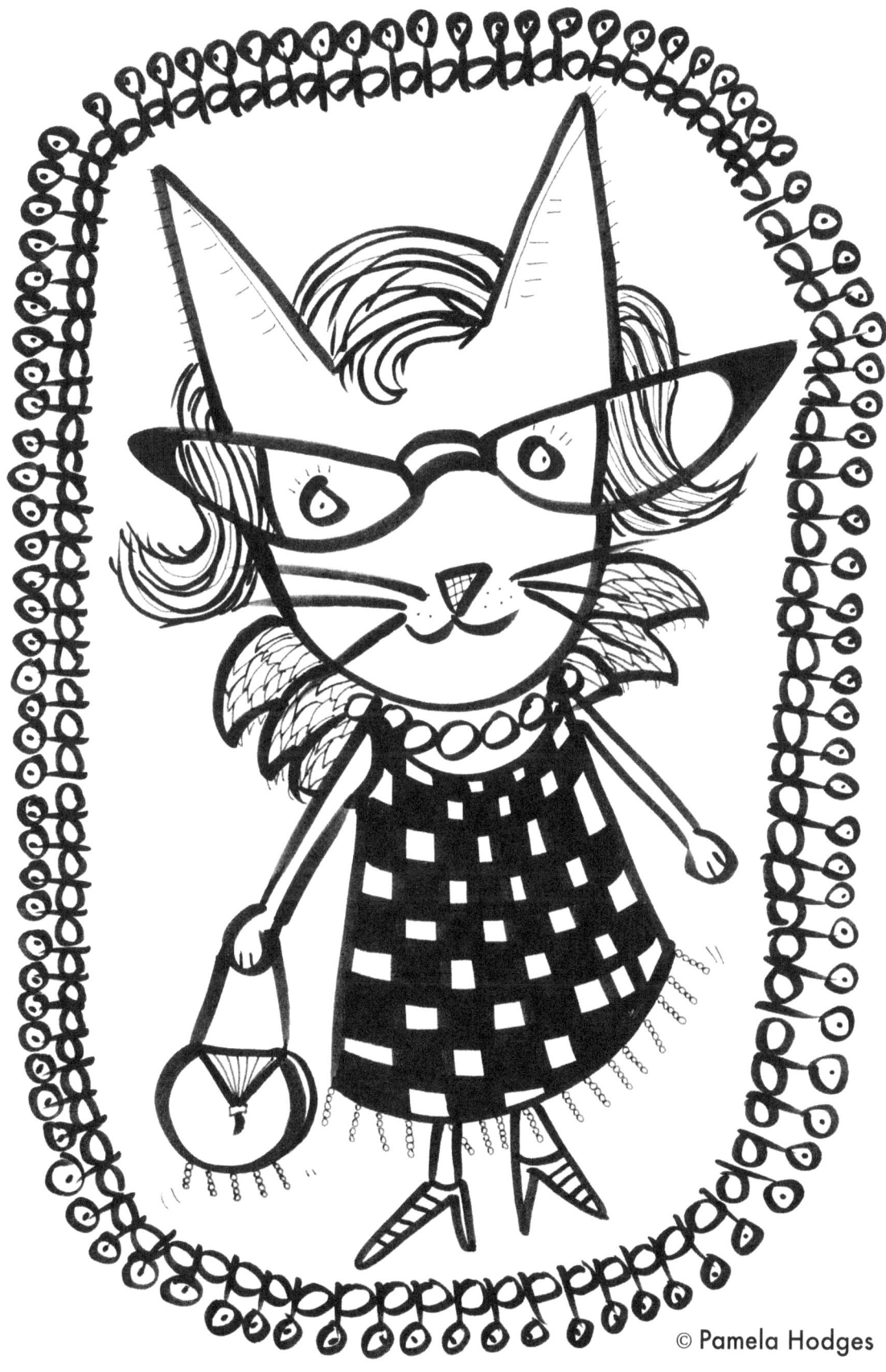

© Pamela Hodges

I was dropped from a car in a very busy intersection in Dallas when I was just a kitten. Luckily, a mommy and daughter in the car right behind me saw what happened and rescued me from the side of the highway. They call me The Beast because I am not always nice. But I still love them.

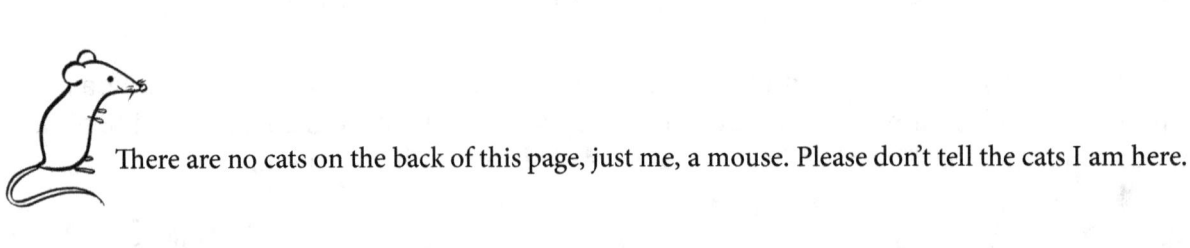 There are no cats on the back of this page, just me, a mouse. Please don't tell the cats I am here.

TIGGIE

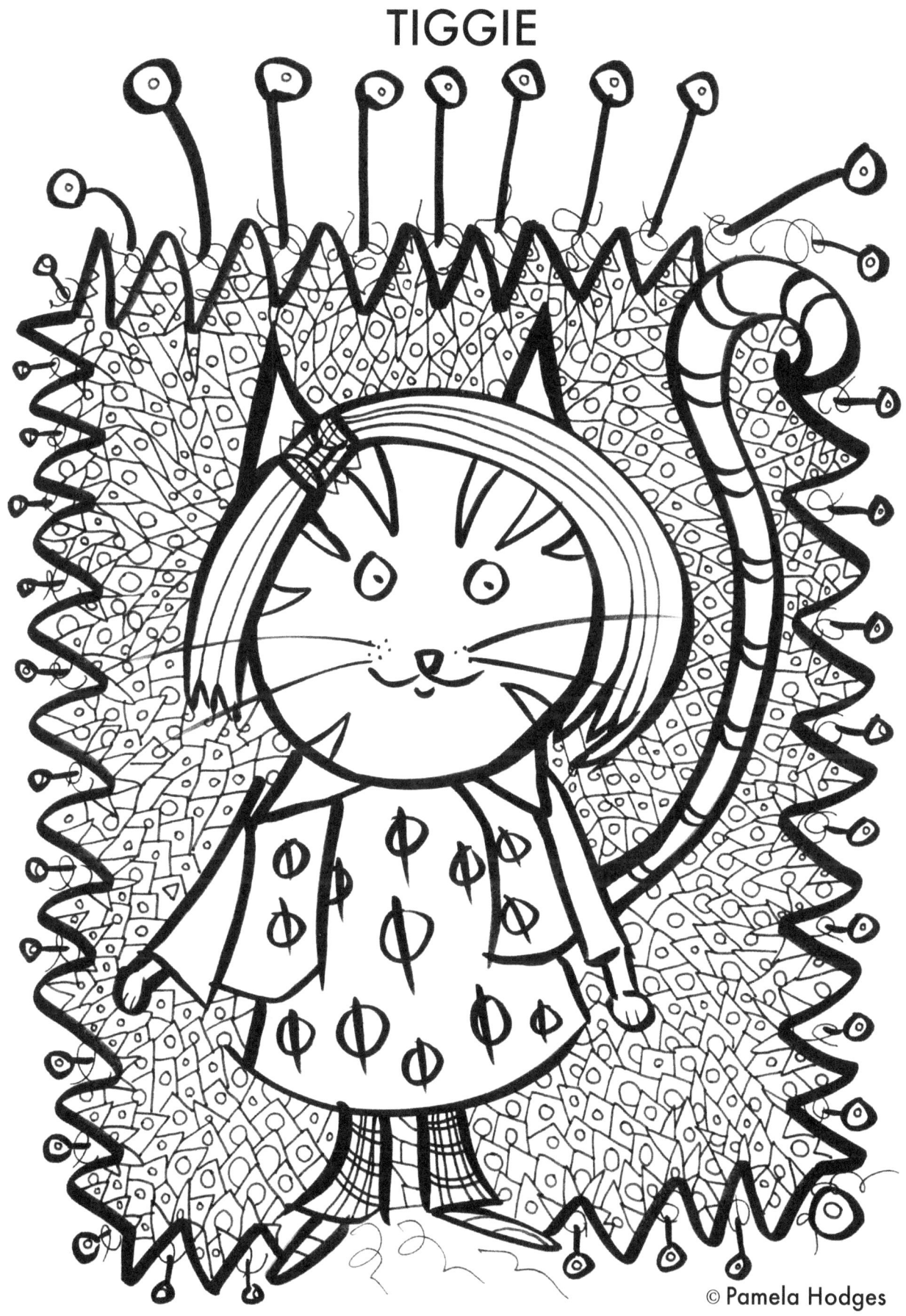

© Pamela Hodges

My name is Tiggie, not Tigger, because I am a girl not a boy. I was born in a barn in Kansas; then I travelled over six hundred miles to Texas to live with this nice lady's daughter-in-law. They always wanted an orange tiger cat. And I always wanted to be loved.

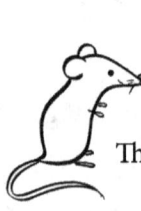 There are no cats on the back of this page, just me, a mouse. Please don't tell the cats I am here.

TIKA

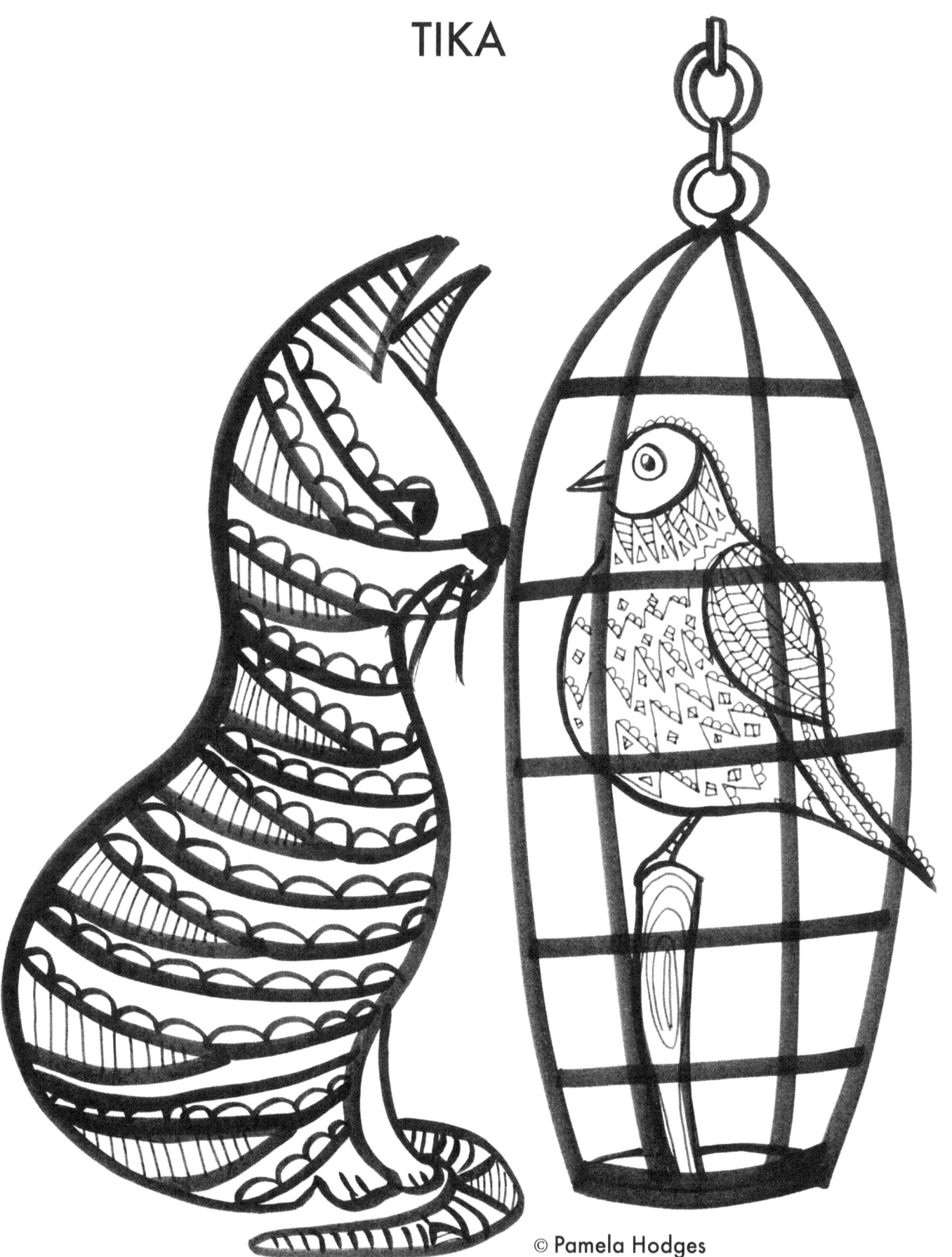

© Pamela Hodges

I came to my family one day in August, when they were home from school. I wandered up to the back door and asked to be let in. When they opened the door, I immediately ran to the food dish. Once they had fed me, I couldn't bear the thought of leaving. I really want to open the door on the parakeet cage.

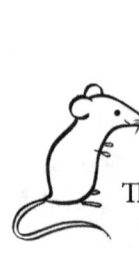 There are no cats on the back of this page, just me, a mouse. Please don't tell the cats I am here.

TRISTAN

© Pamela Hodges

My brother, Beau, and I were adopted together. When our cat mother got pregnant, the homeowners where she lived put her outside and abandoned her. My mother was taken in by a kind neighbor three days before we were born. Now we catch bugs all day and leave them as presents for our human.

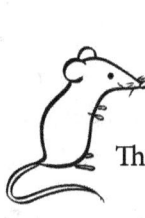 There are no cats on the back of this page, just me, a mouse. Please don't tell the cats I am here.

WALTRUDE

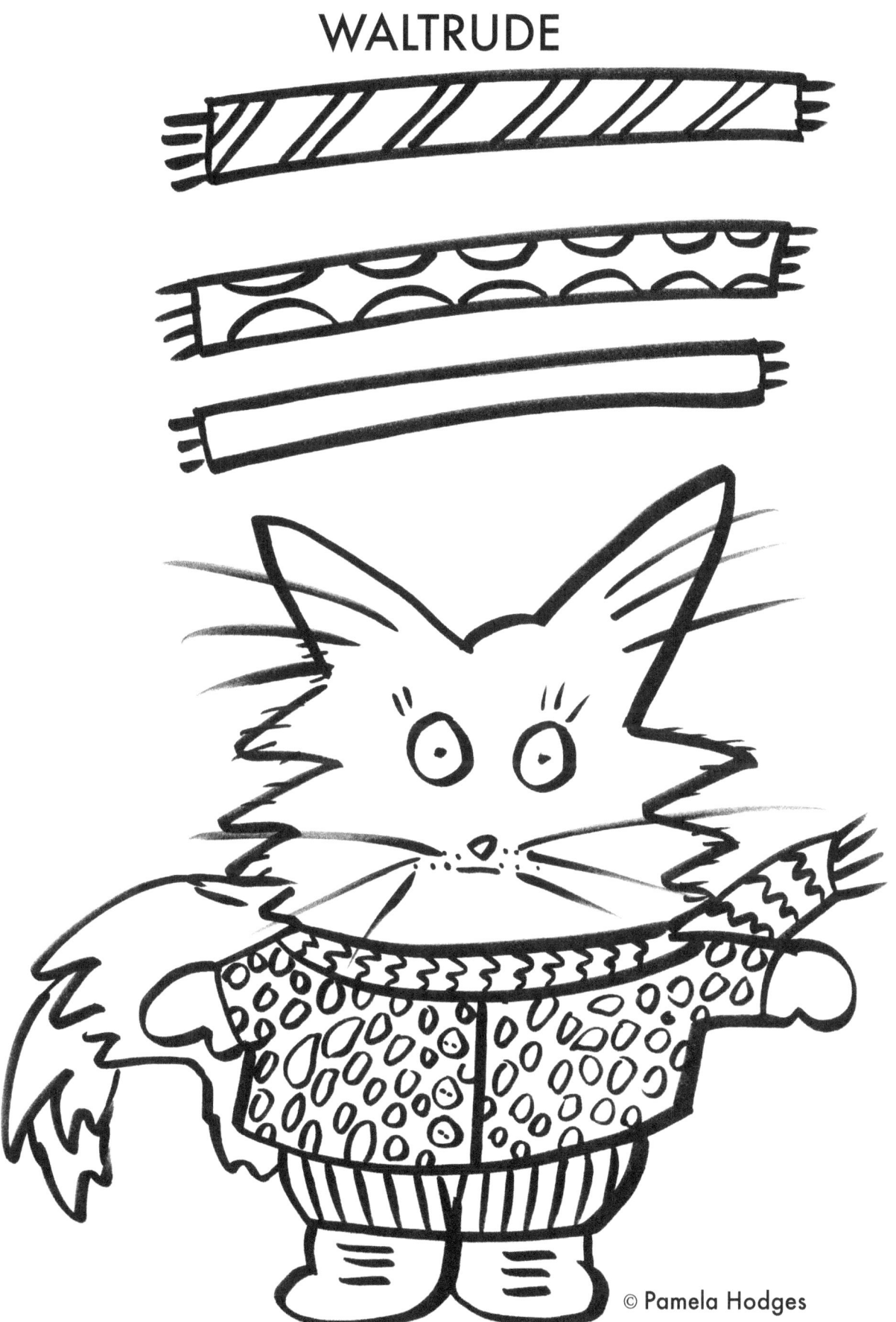

© Pamela Hodges

You can call me Wally; my real name is Walltrude. I was born in a closet. My little sisters died very young. There is just me, my oldest sister, and my mom now. I may be small but I'm very mighty. My favorite TV show is *Sherlock*. Benedict Cumberbatch sure knows how to act!

 There are no cats on the back of this page, just me, a mouse. Please don't tell the cats I am here.

ZOE

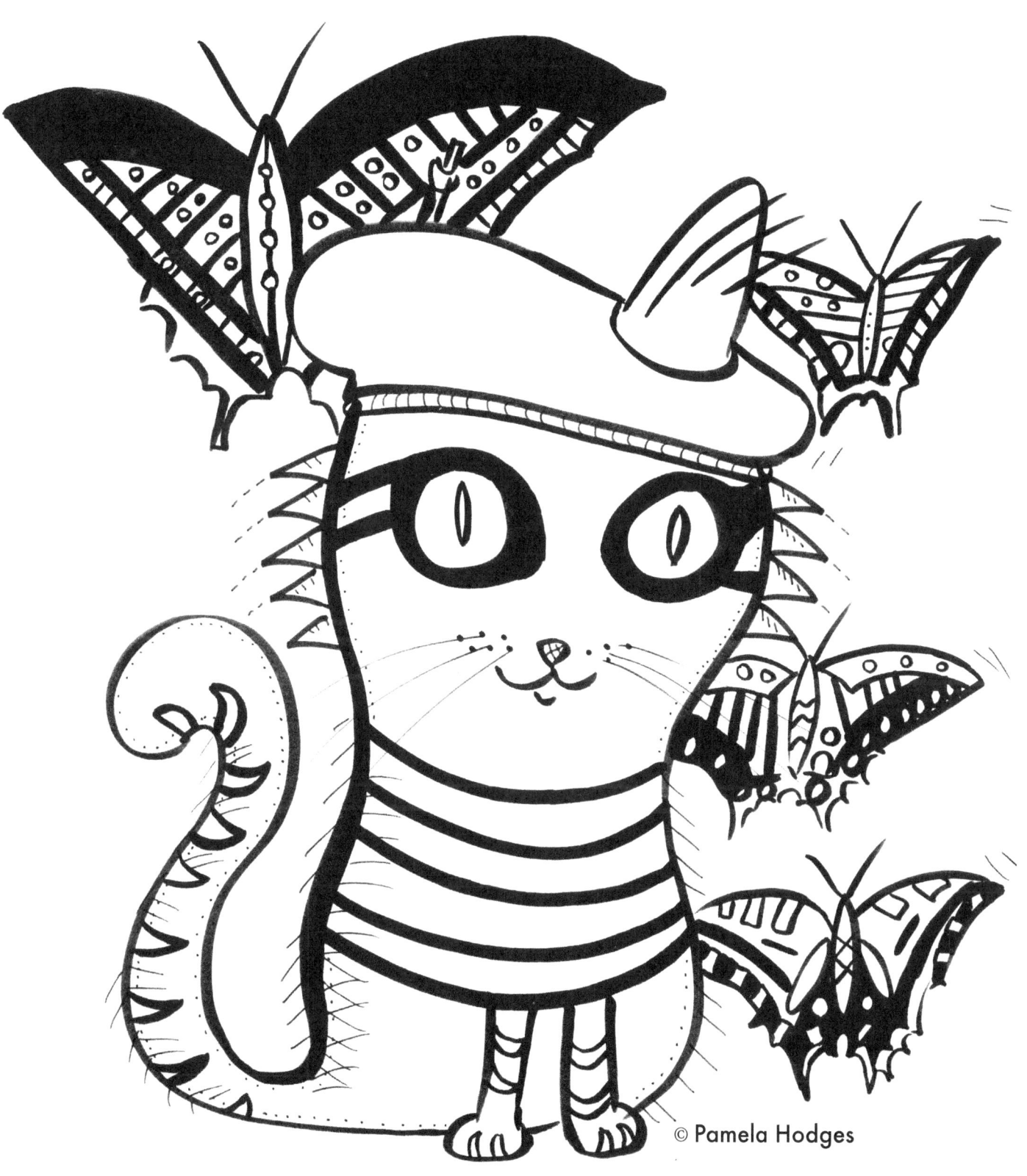

© Pamela Hodges

My name is Zoe. I was found on the streets of a tiny village in France, being taken care of, as best he could, by a homeless man who rescued me from a rubbish dump where I was abandoned as a kitten. That is why I am afraid of bags and like the outdoors. A family adopted me from an animal rescue.

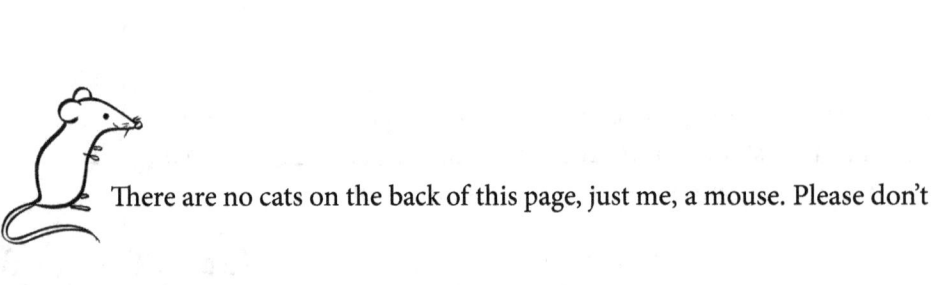 There are no cats on the back of this page, just me, a mouse. Please don't tell the cats I am here.

Acknowledgements

Thank you Annie, Arwen, Bridgett, Buddy, Caspar, Charlie, Cow, Cupcake, Star, Denali, Dot, Fiona, Flea, Flynn, Harper, Harry Truman, Jazz, Joi, Kaner, Larry, Latte, Lilli, Little Bit, Lyra, Mackayla, Milo, Mokka, Patricia, Rupi, Sassy, Skittles, Smokey, Spock, Tardis, The Beast, Tiggie, Tika, Tristan, Waltrude, and Zoe.

Without you, there would be no coloring book.

XO

PAMELA

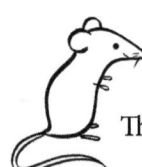 There are no cats on the back of this page, just me, a mouse. Please don't tell the cats I am here.

About the Artist

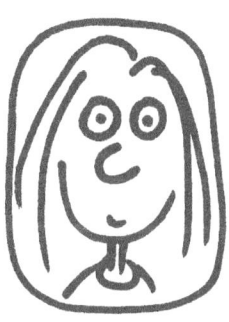

http://www.ipaintiwrite.com
pamela@ipaintiwrite.com
instagram @pamelahodges
twitter @hodgeswriter
facebook@PamelaHodgesWriter

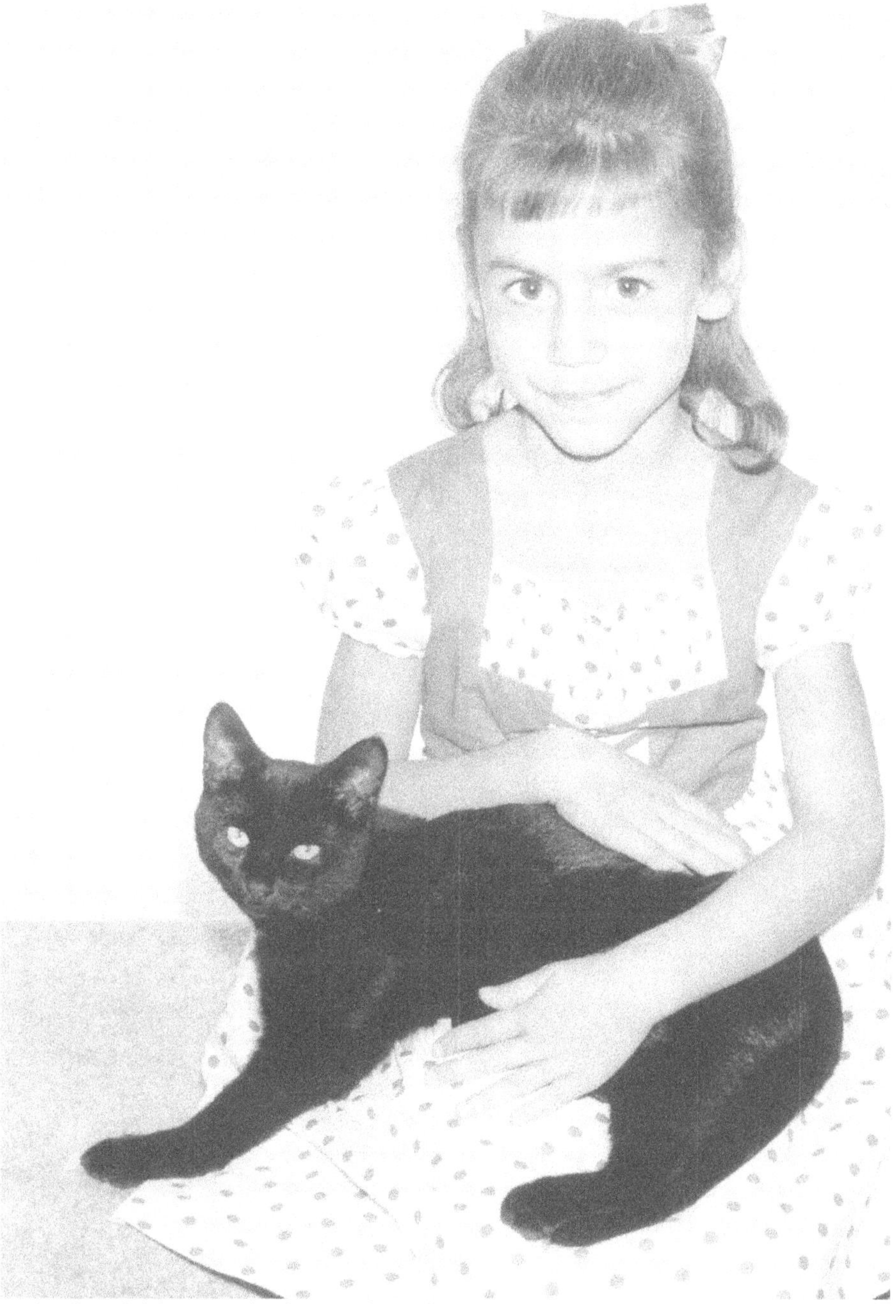

Pamela Hodges and Blacky in 1965, when she was Pamela Fernuik.

Pamela Hodges has scrubbed toilets as a janitor for Sears in Saskatoon Saskatchewan, Canada. She has weeded sugar beets as a volunteer on Kibbutz Reshafim in Israel, and she has worked as a fashion photographer in Tokyo, Japan.

Now she writes, draws, paints, and cleans seven litter boxes. She has one husband, three children, four cats, and two dogs. She lives in Pennsylvania and misses her mom and brother who live in Canada, where she grew up.

Pamela writes about art, creativity and everyday life at ipaintiwrite.com. She encourages you to believe in yourself and your ability to create. She is also the typist for her cat, Harper, who writes about life as a cat at thecatwhowrites.com.

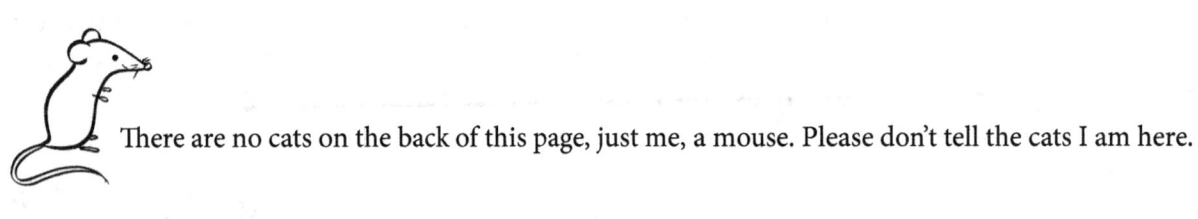 There are no cats on the back of this page, just me, a mouse. Please don't tell the cats I am here.

About the Cat Who Writes

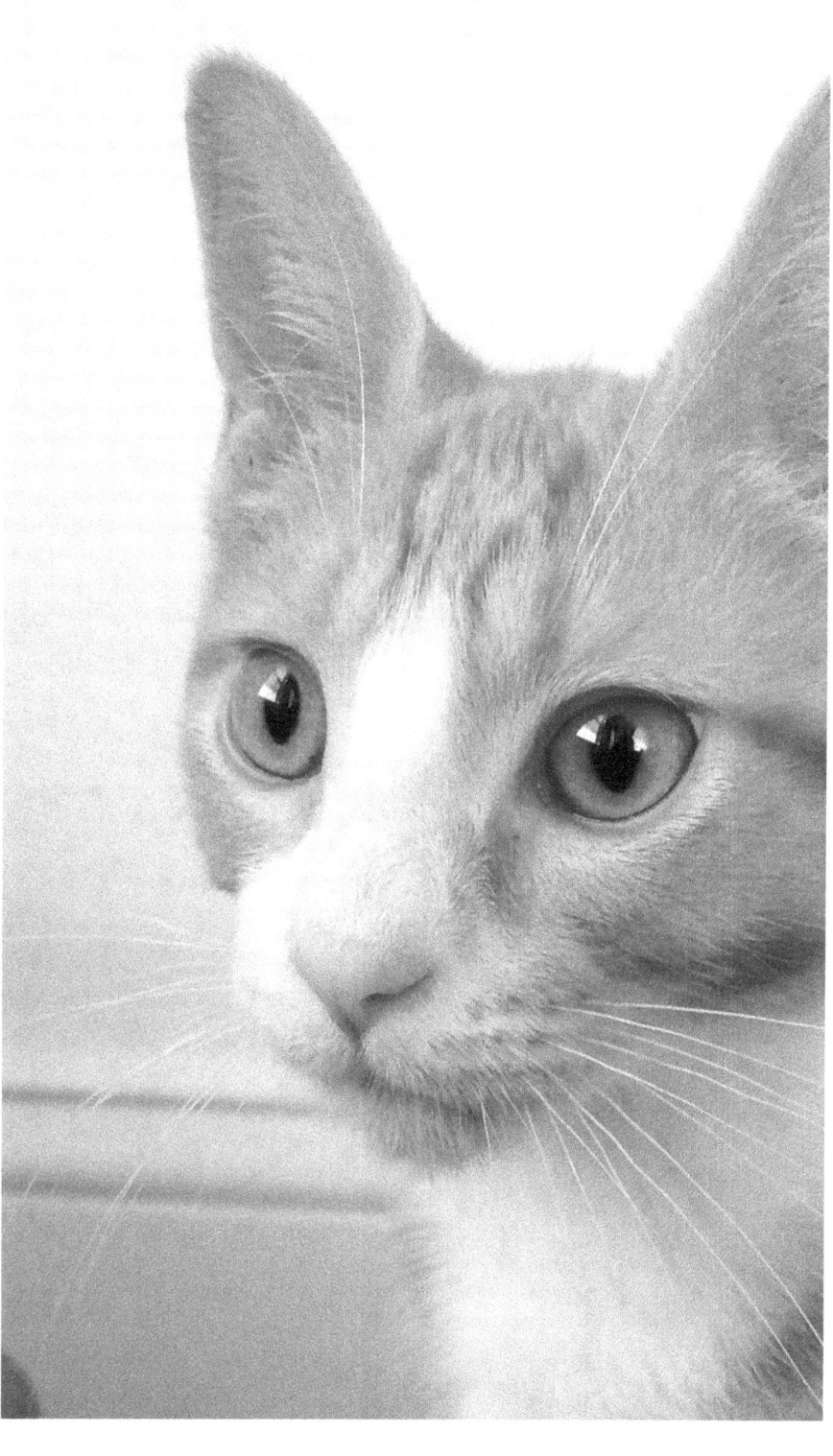

http://www.TheCatWhoWrites.com
TheCatHarper@gmail.com
instagram@TheCatWhoWrites
twitter@TheCatWhoWrites
facebook@TheCatHarper

My typist and rescuer, Pamela Hodges, named me Harper after the writer, Harper Lee. I was born in a barn and abandoned with my brother at an animal rescue. I have no thumbs, so, I dictate and Pamela types for me. I write at TheCatWhoWrites.com.

I am learning how to read. My favorite word is cat. My hobby is to knock everything off of Mrs. Hodges' desk. She still can not find her red pair of glasses. Once I hid her computer mouse for seven days.

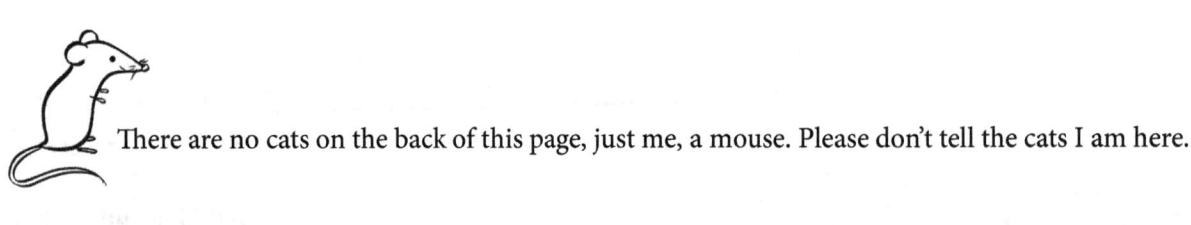
There are no cats on the back of this page, just me, a mouse. Please don't tell the cats I am here.

Draw a cat. Color the cat.

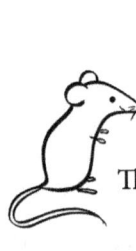 There are no cats on the back of this page, just me, a mouse. Please don't tell the cats I am here.

Draw a cat. Color the cat.

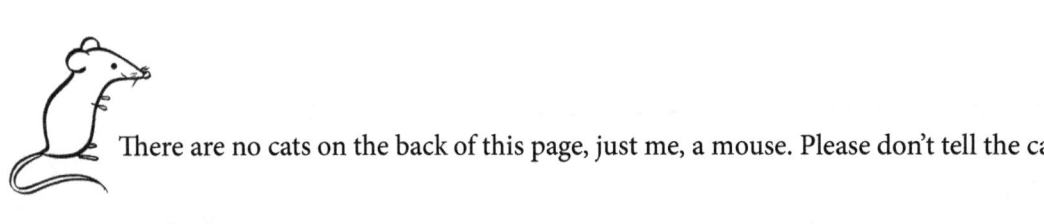 There are no cats on the back of this page, just me, a mouse. Please don't tell the cats I am here.

Draw a cat. Color the cat.